CULTURE CLASH

To Ale Poulter
P.C.C. Christmas 2021

Other books by Adrian L Hawkes

Leadership And …
Published by NLM Publications (First Printing 1987)
Published by New Wine Press (Second Edition/Reprint 1992)

Attracting Training Releasing Youth
Published by New Wine Press (1992)
Published by iUniverse, Inc. (Second Edition/Reprint 2008)

Jacob a Fatherless Generation
Published by Rainbow Publishing (2002)

Hello is that You God
Published by iUniverse, Inc. (New York Lincoln Shanghai) (2007)

Book by Gareth Hawkes and Mark Yates
Poemry we shall replace Poetry
Published by Generation Resources Centre

CULTURE CLASH

A book, a trainer's manual and
a student manual on the subject of culture
FOR CONTINUOUS PROFESSIONAL DEVELOPMENT

Adrian L. Hawkes

iUniverse, Inc.
New York   Bloomington   Shanghai

CULTURE CLASH
A book, a trainer's manual and a student manual on the subject of culture for continuous professional development

Copyright © 2008 by Adrian L. Hawkes

All rights reserved. No part of this book may be used or reproduced by any means, graphic, electronic, or mechanical, including photocopying, recording, taping or by any information storage retrieval system without the written permission of the publisher except in the case of brief quotations embodied in critical articles and reviews.

iUniverse books may be ordered through booksellers or by contacting:

iUniverse
1663 Liberty Drive
Bloomington, IN 47403
www.iuniverse.com
1-800-Authors (1-800-288-4677)

Because of the dynamic nature of the Internet, any Web addresses or links contained in this book may have changed since publication and may no longer be valid.

The views expressed in this work are solely those of the author and do not necessarily reflect the views of the publisher, and the publisher hereby disclaims any responsibility for them.

ISBN: 978-0-595-50707-8 (pbk)
ISBN: 978-0-595-61619-0 (ebk)

Printed in the United States of America

INDEX to THE BOOK

THANKS vii

FOREWORD ix

PREFACE xi

CHAPTER ONE: WHAT IS CULTURE 3

CHAPTER TWO: WHY IS KNOWING ABOUT
                    CULTURE IMPORTANT? 9

CHAPTER THREE: HOW CULTURES ARE FORMED
                    (AND WHO ARE WE?) 15

CHAPTER FOUR: DEFINING A CULTURE 19

CHAPTER FIVE: CULTURAL CHANGE IN OUR WORLD 22

CHAPTER SIX: CULTURE AND THE CHANGE FACTOR 26

CHAPTER SEVEN: CULTURE AND THE ROLE OF WOMEN ... 30

CHAPTER EIGHT: HOW URBANIZATION CHANGES CULTURE ... 34

CHAPTER NINE: THE IMPORTANCE OF META-NARRATIVE ... 37

CHAPTER TEN: OUR PRESUPPOSITIONS 41

CHAPTER ELEVEN: THE CLASH OF CULTURES 44

CHAPTER TWELVE: COMPANY CULTURES 47

THANKS

To Jan Doidge for all her correction work
To Anita Brooks for all her correction work
For Pauline My wife for putting up with me, going on about subjects like culture

CHAPTER ONE

WHAT IS CULTURE

The reality is that if we go next door, and our neighbour is very, very much like us there are nevertheless cultural changes. There will be things that they do differently, ways of thinking, expectations, likes and dislikes that they will have absorbed from different areas of life that have made them what they are. However, because these are often small things we hardly know the difference and maybe don't even think about those things.

Some of the easy things to spot that reflect cultural changes are things like dress and food. Then there are things like music and art that help to define a culture; then of course there are the big things like what is important: what is the value system of the culture we are looking at? Sometimes those things are a little harder to grasp.

So, by way of example, I originally come from Birmingham. For those of you who know the UK you will know that that area of the country has its own distinctive Midlands accent, which is accentuated by its flat vowel sounds.

When we move away from our home area those local accents tend to get affected by where we lived; apart from my journalist friend Dan Wooding who has live for 30 years in California USA and still has a strong Brummie accent, as if he had only moved across the pond a week ago. I reckon he cultivates it for the benefit of his business contacts!

However, I have lived in quite a few places and so my accent has changed; though, if you listen carefully you can still hear those flat 'a' and 'o' sounds and the like, but it's not so strong. When visiting my Mother, who still lives in Birmingham, I asked her if she had always had a Birmingham accent. She replied in surprise, telling me that she did not have any kind of accent! I asked her why she thought that, she said simply, well I went next door and asked them if I had an accent and they said 'No, of course you don't!'

So, what is culture? Well, generally it is that which a large group of people think is normal, whatever normal is. It is all sorts of things: dress, religion, food, marriage expectations, work, approach to children, the way business is conducted, music, advertising art, drama, the expectations of life now and into the hereafter, in fact everything!

And where does this thing I/we are calling culture come from?

Someone said to me recently "Well surely culture comes from our family". I think that is only partly right. The family itself is pressured, moved, moulded and made by all sorts of other external pressures. They are what I call the 'four legs of a table',—that which holds the table up—but in the terms of what we are discussing they do more than hold it up; they actually create the shape of the table. They are the cultural makers and changers.

Before I continue, whilst I am putting them down as four, we need to be aware that the 'legs' (if you will let me call them that) are often interchangeable, inter-influential and impacting each other and of course impacting the family and so the greater community or culture.

These four 'legs' are as follows:

Business or 'economics'.

That is a powerful moulder and often one that we might not consider. We need to know that our economics are very powerful in terms of how we feel and act, and how we respond to others; shaping our goals and visions, or lack of them. If you have no food in your stomach and no roof over your head it wonderfully concentrates the mind as to what you want to do next. It will tend to affect all your actions and reactions. That will, of course, mould and make us and, if we are part of a whole community where resources are generally scarce, then that will affect all sorts of things.

I am fascinated by the story in the Bible where Moses rescued the children of Egypt from slavery, and promises them freedom. What on earth does freedom mean to such people; indeed, what does slavery mean? Slavery for them was the norm. It was the culture; they were slaves! The family to the right of them were slaves; the family to the left of them were slaves; the family across the road, if they had a road, were also slaves!

This was their culture; this was their normality! What was this strange freedom that mad Moses was talking about? In fact, we get a glimpse of just how difficult it was for them to comprehend this when they start complaining that Moses had brought them to the desert to kill them. It seems they were asked what they themselves wanted and they were very clear about it; they said they were ok in Egypt! OK? What did they mean by OK?

Well, they said: 'there we had cucumbers, leeks and onions and the occasional fish!' They didn't want freedom. It was not part of the culture—onions and leeks were! (The Bible: Numbers Chapter 11 Verse 5)[i]. You can read the whole story around chapter 11 of Numbers.

So do economics and business mould the culture, assuredly they do!

Art and Media

Then, another leg of the table would be what I have generally labelled 'Art and Media'. Into that would go all our television programmes, advertising, both print media and electronic, theatre, hoardings (billboards), books and papers; in fact all those things that are designed to persuade us. Do they? Well, of course they do! That is why advertisers pay such large amounts to tell us what they want us to know and think and how they feel we should act. They understand that to mould culture can be very profitable to those who know how to do it. I watched a T.V. programme once where they where trying to assess how much advertising affects us. They asked an audience how much they thought they were affected by advertising; most said they were not affected by it. Then the presenter asked people which petrol they used in their car by choice. He presented four brands; they audience responded. I noted that one brand had the most response, and then the responses tailed off for the other three. It turned out that the majority of people had chosen the brand that spent the most on advertising; the next largest amount of people chose the brand that had the second largest amount of marketing spend and so on for all four brands. But this was supposedly a group of people who where not persuaded by advertising!!

Do these medias mould our culture? I think so!

Politics, government and religion

On to leg number three, 'Politics, government and religion'. Why have I put those three together? Well, let's try and divide them first. Government, I see as the big picture. National, European, and International governments all have moulding effects. Sometimes those effects take a long time to filter down. I live in London; some people in the provinces say 'oh well, that's a London thing; we live here it doesn't affect us'; however what you find is that in the UK governments think in a certain way, decisions are made, laws are passed and the first area to be affected is London, but give it time and those effects filter across the country and gradually change the whole culture. The reality is that change is a process, so when a law is passed it does not immediately affect peoples opinions … but give it time. If the USA is the dominant culture we could look there for changes that will ultimately affect the UK. I remember smiling to myself when multi-channel TV came to the USA and people on the limited UK media where laughing at it saying, 'that's there, it won't come here'.

How naive!

Then, of course, the government has the power to affect economics, justice issues and social factors and though we may say that politics is boring, it still is affecting and changing our lives and we disengage from it at our peril.

Politics! What is that? Well here is one dictionary definition (there are others): *the total complex of relations between people living in society.* Using that definition, that politics could be the local group meeting in a community centre, or the church board, or the social group that comes together to make decisions on behalf of a community. We all do it at sometime or another; and it affects things and changes things.

Why Religion? Well, it seems to me that from time immemorial government has often used religion to influence, change and control people groups, nationally and internationally. Often, government leaders will pay lip service to a religion so that control is brought to bear on a population. Think about Constantine (first ever Christian Roman Emperor) to start with. (27th Feb 272 to 22nd May 337). We must not mistake the religion used by the state as the 'reality', that would be a gross mistake, but does it influence things? The state's intervention with religion is why we in the UK live with the Church of England (28 June 1491–28 January 1547). Several significant pieces of legislation were enacted during Henry VIII's reign. They included the several Acts which severed the

English Church from the Roman Catholic Church and established Henry as the supreme head of the Church in England; the Laws in Wales Acts 1535–1542, which brought the law in Wales in line with that in England and the Buggery Act 1533, the first anti-sodomy enactment in England. Do these things affect the culture and the way we live? Of course they do!

Education

Then there is the fourth leg of the table, and that's what I have labelled Education. Such a powerful one, as those of you who have had small children will know! Those five year olds come home and you say 'this is how you do your homework', and they say 'not so, my teacher says it's like this', and teacher wins! Of course, Education is more than going to school. Education is life ... and family ... local community ... culture as a whole will all have an effect. To quote an African proverb: *It takes a whole village to bring up a child.* And so it does.

I am often attacked by people because I have established, and still help to run, Christian schools. People suggest I am influencing those young people to think in a certain way. Some rude people even go so far as to say I am brain washing them! I am equally strong in my response: 'Yes! Of course I am ... what do you think the other lot are doing?'! The reality is that there is no such thing as objective, clean sheet, education. All of it is biased, culturally influenced, and has passed on a cultural value system both good and bad; indeed it still continues to do so. To all those teachers out there who think I am allowing the children in my care to make their own decisions without my influence on them I have to say that is unthinking balderdash.

One guy, who was a Christian but somewhat cynical about Christian schools, said to me: "How ridiculous to think you can teach English or Maths in a Christian way. That's silly, it's just English; it's just Maths." Oh, really? One young lady in my care left the Christian school at 16 and went to a local college. One day she showed me her homework. It was simply an English exercise to put in capital letters, commas and full stops.

The sentence read, *'on arrival home I discovered my boyfriend in bed with a friend of mine.'* Correct the grammar! No influence, amoral; not a value system in sight. Not culturally influential, objective or without bias? I don't think so!

So, that's the cultural table—and each one of those legs moulds it, makes it and holds it up. And if you have a view and you want to change the culture or influence it, you can only do it by engaging with those important areas. You cannot opt out, and even if you think you have, the culture is affecting you more than you know, as we shall see!

The culture is, of course, changing all the time because of the effect of those 'legs'. What are the biggest moulders currently? I would say it is film … TV … the soaps … and most of it is American made. We all watch, listen and are affected by it; so that becomes the universal dominant culture. Naturally it will be regionally affected, but the big picture is that the USA, through media, is influencing culture throughout the world. That also can lead to real opposition, sometimes rightly, as can be seen by various radicals world wide.

CHAPTER TWO
WHY IS KNOWING ABOUT CULTURE IMPORTANT?

In this current century more and more people live in urban conurbations, and those cities are generally becoming multi-cultural to a huge extent. Travelling on the tube into the city of London I am struck by the incredible variety of languages I may hear on any one trip. Figures for one part of London near me showed that there were 44 different languages spoken in the area with no dominant group. The way in which we are living amongst each other in an unprecedented way means there is a great need to understand each other imposed upon us. We cannot help but bump into each other and interact, even if we do often retreat into our own cultural ghettoes.

Often, misunderstanding could be avoided if our understanding was greater:

A friend of mine from Sweden, who lived for a long time in the UK, came into the office one day and said:

"Oh dear I have just done a terrible thing, and I realised what I had done but no simple explanation could adjust it".

"What was that?" I asked?

"Well," she went on, "I was in the post office and accidentally bumped into a lady. I immediately said sorry, but having just returned from Sweden I forgot that the inflection in English must go at the end of the word and I put the rise in sound in the middle. The lady assumed immediately that what I was saying by my sorry, was that it was her fault, which I did not mean and she was really angry ... I knew what I had done wrong, but it was too difficult to explain in such a situation."

Just think, if there had been mutual understanding the outcome would have been so different, and that was such a small incident. Imagine the bigger ones!

When we live in a culture that is fairly mono-culture (by which I mean a culture where we do not notice large changes) then we very rarely think about culture. We certainly don't know why we do what we do and wouldn't blame culture. We assume that our thinking, actions and prejudices, are all normal; and usually we don't think about those things at all. So, this book and course is all about making people THINK about their own culture. If we do that often enough it will create change in us. Change first of all in our thinking, and then … the sky is the limit! Some things about our culture, all of our cultures, will be good, some will be amoral, and some things will be downright bad. Unless we think about the whys and the wherefores nothing will change and some of these things ought to—especially those things we perceive as bad.

Much of the course section of this book is delivered to people who are involved in counselling others; or to those who will be come foster carers for others.

Having delivered this course in many areas of the UK I have noted how people suddenly discover things that they had made assumptions on, and drawn conclusions on, concerning other people that they had touched, sometimes professionally.

One lady surprised me as she had been in contact with a Ghanaian young man on a professional basis. I explained that in West African culture to look a person in the eyes when they are older than you when in conversation would show disrespect to the older person. The lady was amazed. She explained that she was about to give up on the young man she had been working with because, as he never looked her in they eye, she thought he was shifty. Now she understood that the young man was actually being respectful to her and was encouraged to continue to try to help him.

It's all about understanding! The way that others arrive at what they do, or their conclusions, may not be the same ours. We need to understand the starting point and realise that although the premise that has been arrived at may not be what we expected, it may not be wrong—just different.

I have tried to paint a picture as to how culture is influenced and changed and how it is formed; in other words where it comes from, what it is, what makes and changes it.

To take this further we need to understand what effect all that is having on us as individuals, us as families, and us as communities and nations. If you listen carefully you hear even national governments asking culturally related questions. Things like: Why is crime on the increase? Why is there such family break down? What is happening to increase truancy and drop out in our school systems? These are culturally related questions.

In asking the question what makes the culture, we are also asking the question what makes me. How have we got here both as individuals and as a group? What effect does the culture have on the family and the individual that we need to understand and, if we came to a correct understanding, would we do some things differently, a little like my Swedish friend and the Ghanaian?

We, I hope, have already agreed that culture is not static, but is constantly changing. It would probably help us if we were to understand some of the changes that have taken place and thus produced 'the now'. We might be very surprised how far those effects go back. We are always reaping the results of history. If we can understand the things that have changed us and affected us, and brought us to our current situation, surely we will be in a better position to understand what is going on both personally and how, by our understanding, we might help others.

Let's just recap on the big things that are changing us at the moment, such as film and TV. Not to forget the other electronic media such as phone and computers. Did you know, for example, that in one country there was a revolution created just by people texting each other? (*"Text messaging toppled Joseph Estrada in Filipinas": Eric Ellis, Time Asia*) Well, that changed things didn't it!

But how about the historical things that have changed us, what are they?

According to PEPA[ii] (Practical Effective Performing Arts) which for a time was the arts group in the church of which I am a part, there were major historical events over the last few decades that brokered the changes, and they have for each decade been given a sort of label. For the 40s decade they used the label WAR and of course it was, right through until the 50s (at least from a UK perspective).

After the war came the 50s and for this they gave the label EXPECTATION. Again we can understand why they would put that label on. A time of world war was over and there was an expectation of better things. I grew up in the 50s and it certainly was a time in which possibilities arose. In my area everyone got a TV in 1953 to watch the coronation. All sorts of new things where driving a cultural expectation.

Then there was the 60s—a time of REVOLUTION: peace and love man! 'Let's make love, not war' was the slogan. Freedom, which most of us didn't really understand (and still often don't understand), was a powerful cultural changer, and it probably still is deeply affecting the way we live now.

After the 60s, as the teens of that time grew up to find that peace, love, free sex and drugs didn't make a better world, there came a time of DISSILUSIONMENT. Their philosophy of freedom didn't work. Many of the freedom seekers ended up in 9 to 5 jobs, married with a mortgage, and joined the rat race they had so despised. No wonder they were disillusioned!

There probably could be some argument about the 80s as it is not so far away from us, but PEPA used the label SELFISHNESS. Key words from that decade where things like look after number one; some of that is still with us. Or, consider the famous Mrs Thatcher's phrase, 'there is no such thing as community'. Then there were the 90s, what was that all about? The PEPA group labelled that decade DESPAIR; were they right? New Musical Express, which was very big in the 90s, reported that suicide increased in that decade. the result of extreme selfishness is despair. We cannot live as if we were on an island by ourselves. That's desperate; we need others!

Whatever Mrs Thatcher, said we need community!

Each of those centuries have had a moulding effect on the current culture. What about the 00s? Well we are up to 2006 at the time of writing. PEPA didn't give our current decade a label, it was too early. Maybe mine might be one of FEAR, on an international scale. Fear on the streets, fear of extremism, and fear of fanaticism. Maybe I will revise that thinking, but it certainly is having its cultural effects, even in terms of obesity. How often do you hear parents say "the streets are too unsafe, I have to drive my children to school"? That is a general cultural action, a big change.

Although we can see that each century brings about change, nevertheless changes in culture are sometimes slower than we think. They go back further than we really know. So, in reality although we are closer to the 80s and 90s the real big changes that are affecting us today were really started in the 40s, and we are reaping their effects now. Think about those big changes. Before World War Two, women did not go out to work. The war created a necessity that they did, and when the war was over they couldn't be put back into the box. That was, and is, a massive cultural change. In fact it has continued to evolve and change thinking and culture right through to the present.

Economics, remember that cultural leg, are of course having an affect as housing needs demand that all who can earn do so; to contribute to the family roof. Are these changes affecting us as individuals, communities, and the wider culture? I think so, don't you?

I have called the current generations 'the Fatherless generation'. All around the world there are fatherless children; there are orphans in greater number than there has ever been. These orphans are created by huge pressures. Some, as in the West, are orphans, because of the break down of traditional family; cultural changes so big that we sometimes find a child in a family where neither the Father nor the Mother is the birth parents. I am not now talking about natural orphans through death, or those in the care system; these are children whose parents split up.

The Mother may have had custody of the children and then married again, or even died, and now Father number two is left and remarries. The child is actually not biologically related to either but is yet in 'the family'. This presents immense challenges.

Then, in some countries, war has created an inordinate amount of orphans. There is a shortage of men; some places I have been you hardly see young men—they have either emigrated, are dead or are still fighting a war. The end product is the same huge amount of fatherless children.

In Africa, the traditional culture was that when someone died and left orphans the extended family swung into action and the child became a member of a new family. With the advent of AIDS this has caused such pressure on that cultural norm that there is a breakdown of that expectation and children are left to their own devices, and, without governmental resources to do anything, they are left to roam—a truly fatherless generation. These things are creating huge international cultural changes, and we do not yet know where they will lead us.

CHAPTER THREE

HOW CULTURES ARE FORMED (AND WHO ARE WE?)

The fact is that cultures are becoming almost generic, and we are, on a world wide basis subject to world pressure on local culture—'the global village effect', no less. Some are nevertheless discovering their cultural identity that they thought they had lost. So, in some areas, there is a revival of language and an attempt to discover original culture; and a desire to go back to what was—such as the Maori in New Zealand, or the Welsh and Scottish people in the United Kingdom.

Whilst I personally think such movements are interesting, I do, however, think that it is quite hard to put the genie back in the bottle and the generic effect of the global village is affecting us all even if we want to rediscover the past. I have travelled for all sorts of reasons most of my life. In my opinion one of the most interesting things was the different way things were done; the huge difference in things you could buy in different countries. Now you wouldn't say that had all gone, but so many airport lounges have the same goods, and the big shops have the same goods in the big cities. Even the food is becoming generic. Perhaps that is because I live in London and am influenced by the fact that I cannot think of any nation's food that is not available at a London restaurant.

One of the strange things to me now is that I can watch almost the same TV programmes whatever country I am in.

Sometimes they come with subtitles; in the richer countries they are sometimes dubbed into the local language. That's funny too, to watch certain American cowboys speaking in drawling French, it doesn't quite seem right somehow!

The reality is that we get our culture from such sources, and if we are all watching the same things that has a universal effect on the 'norm'. We are therefore beginning to perceive the 'norm' the same wherever we are, and although Bollywood is probably producing just as many films as Hollywood, nevertheless Hollywood has the universal world distribution.

Who we are, to some extent, is defined by the culture we live in. It gives us the meaning of self. If we are too far removed from what is perceived to be the norm, then we become outsiders and that can be quite difficult, even painful. The problem is that to progress, innovate and discover, in fact for all the entrepreneurial skills, people need to move away from the norm; to get out of the box. That can ultimately benefit others; but it is not easy to do. Often such people are considered odd or just plain wrong. Most of those in the business world who started with great innovation where considered crazy. Apparently, when Henry Ford first borrowed money from the bank to set up his car factory, an accountant asked the banker if he should buy shares in the enterprise. The banker said, 'No it's ridiculous; it won't catch on! Don't lose your money!

Apparently the accountant didn't listen. He bought shares and became a multi-millionaire! You can nevertheless see that the entrepreneur, on this occasion the maker of Ford cars, was considered, probably by many, to be just plain crazy; on the outside of the norm; not fitting into the culture.

So, if our cultural position is so important to us, and it usually is, then who are we? That is a more complicated question than many of us would think. Our culture persuades us to think and act in certain ways that are considered 'normal', and that 'normal' is itself constantly being subject to change. Often though, the change is taking place via small incremental steps, so that we almost do not notice it. In fact, when cultures go through rapid change then that increases pressure on all of us and can create stress. In the past two decades, particularly in the Western World, we have experienced quick and large changes. Much of these have been due to technological changes greater than have been experienced in hundreds of years previously. This increases anxiety in all of us. One only has to think of the experiences that many older people went though when, in the UK, the currency changed from an imperial to a decimal system. The younger you are, of course, the easier it is to cope, but suddenly you are experiencing a seismic shift on what you considered to be normal. There are still people 20 to 30 years on who are still struggling with that change.

Our culture persuades us to think in a certain way, but in reality some of the ways we think are far older than many of us know.

In fact many of you would be surprised to learn that much of our core thinking about basic things like religion and education go back to the early Roman era, and it isn't Roman thinking that influences us but it is Greek thinking that the Romans brought with them throughout the would that they conquered. This thinking was then passed to the rest of the world in colonial times, because most of the colonial powers had originally been conquered by Rome[iii].

I still believe that a culture comes into being by the four pillars that hold it up and which make it and shape it. As I have already mentioned, in broad brush stokes, the four pillars are Education, Media, Politics and Business. If you don't have food, clothing and shelter that affects, in a very important way, how you think and act. Obviously! That will be directly impinged on by business so, if that is in the hands of the few and they don't have good attitudes to the whole, then there will be problems.

If the politicians of the day, those who control the levers of power, do things that create difficulty for the greater part of a population then that will have a moulding effect on the whole. We are changed and influenced by these things and, according to Maslow's Pyramid of Need[iv], these basic things build to the more advanced; but the basics of food, water and shelter must be met before we even start to mould or make the higher things like art or education. Of needs, the bottom areas of warmth, food and clothing are amongst the most basic. It seems to me obvious that those things will affect our cultural expectations and actions in a very profound way.

One of the things that we are witnessing in our world today is the breakdown of some of the larger states and control sectors like the USSR and the former Yugoslavia and, to some extent, the conflict in Iraq. What happens, and what is happening, is that when these control sectors break down, and secrets are revealed that have, for short periods, tried to formulate a national culture, then the society breaks down into its 'tribes'. Really this is a much smaller national identity, or ethnic identity. It really is the extension of 'large family'. Often this group will have been the place where cultural acceptable behaviour has been learnt and where, when the larger control is removed, the group falls back to. As we have seen this is not the recipe for greater stability and peace but rather the increase of cultural conflicts and clashes. It's my tribe against everyone else.

Dr Patrick Dixon[v] has written much more about this subject, here is his comment from a recent article; *All terrorism is extreme tribalism, fuelled by perceived injustice. Unless governments sort out the growing gap between the wealthiest and the poorest nation, they are likely to see new protest movements become terrorist groups.*[vi] Recent television has also been examining the tribal phenomena. It's not new: it's as old as humanity, almost.

So, to summarise so far: who are we? It's always going to be a complicated question. Our upbringing; how we are affected by politics, media, education; our ability to acquire food and shelter; the pressure from those around us, our peers, particularly when growing up and most of all that inherent Greek thinking that has been instilled in us over centuries all contribute to who we are now.

Perhaps, if we understand why we are what we are, and how we came to be so, and if, after our analysis we think there are things wrong; then perhaps we will be willing to take the daring steps of change.

CHAPTER FOUR
DEFINING A CULTURE

How do we define a culture? Well that depends. Often we don't. We don't define it when the people around us are much like us, and that can mean many things: skin colour, accents, dress style, house style, use of things like cars or donkeys, in fact, where lots of people have lots of things just like us, then I have often found that people do not even talk about culture. Rather, things like culture are defined in terms of 'normality' or 'what everyone does'. That, of course, can be a dangerous thing, especially when a community gets an influx of people from another culture. Then, because they are different and are from an unknown culture having different norms, they can often be ostracised, even attacked, and sometimes resented; just because they are different.

Living in a very multi-racial, multi-ethnic multi-everything area I am always aware that I am surrounded by different cultures. My next door neighbours one side speak Russian and the other side speak the dialect from Kerala in India. I am aware that there are cultural expressions and expectations and differences pressing in on me all the time. What is normal becomes a difficult question to answer. My friend Phil Enloe, who is from the USA, would highlight English pronunciation as having the same problem. He is from the mid west of America and asks which way is right 'to-may-tow' or 'To-mar-tow' (for tomato), Lorry or Truck, Boot or Trunk, Hood or Bonnet, Billfold or Wallet? Well, he draws the conclusion that whichever you use locally, that's the right one!

So, if we define a culture it will often be the definition that we think is the 'local norm'.

One of the things that we do need to be well aware of, and often aren't, is that 'local norm' is probably more useful than normal, or, worse still, probably more useful than right! Often it has been my experience that 'right' and 'wrong' don't fit well into the discussion on definitions of culture. Rather, it would be better to acknowledge that this is the way we do it; that is that way you do it. Not right, not wrong, just different!

I have involvement with many churches, and I work quite a lot with Tamil churches in Switzerland and France. The funny thing is that the Swiss always point out to me what is wrong in the way Tamils do things. Meetings start when they start and finish when they finish; and if you are in a German area that must be wrong because Germanic meetings always start and end at a specified time. The clock is in charge and woe betide anyone who breaks the time lord's law! However, because I am white—the same colour as most Swiss people—they assume that I will be sympathetic to their interpretation! Imagine the shock, then, when one young lady, one amongst many I should add, explained to me how wrong this situation was.

I replied, "Yes I am the same colour as you; however I do not come from the same culture. Do you know what I would really like to do when I am in Switzerland?"

"No what is that" she asked.

"Well" I said, sadly, "very bad I know but I would like to make the trains late and throw litter on the floor." She was horrified!

In defining a culture we often think of community, where we live, people in the local vicinity, people we know and people like us. It is, though, important to talk about the culture of organisations, the culture of a company, a hospital, a school, a police force, a political party. All of these areas of collative human endeavour end up with a culture. Sometime it's a helpful culture, sometimes it is anything but. Usually, almost always, no-one sits down and rights a manual of the company culture. Sometimes it may happen, but usually it's those unwritten things that it seems everyone does. Where did it come from? Why is it there? How did it get like that? And the most difficult question … How do we change it if we want to … and can we?

Of course, as I will repeat many times, culture is not static; it is constantly changing; moving on. Sometimes slowly, sometimes in rapid lurches; often without our awareness or understanding; usually defined only as we look back. Just a few take the trouble to try and look at the future and where it will go like my friend Dr Patrick Dixon. Not an easy thing to do. Some, for both good and ill, attempt to manipulate a culture for reasons that suit them, sometimes altruistically, sometimes with evil intent; and usually without the awareness of any great mass of people! Is understanding culture and how we get it and define it important? You bet ya!

CHAPTER FIVE
CULTURAL CHANGE IN OUR WORLD

Cultural change in our world? Of course culture is changing, sometime imperceptibly. I refer you back to what I said in Chapter two about the various changes through the decades, and the reasons for those changes.

Change is affected by all sorts of things: war changes culture; that was one of the major reasons in the UK that the role of women changed. Sure the pressure groups had their place, but the major fact that ladies where required to work in factories during the war because the men where on the battlefield, changed forever the perception in the UK as to what women did or could do. Go to a big company like Cadburys Chocolate before the war and there was a cultural understanding that if you got married you would, OF COURSE, cease to work, and so the director of the company would make a speech and, generally, a presentation. In Cadburys case a flower and a Bible were presented and the chairman would wish the departing female employee all the best for the future in her married life. From then on a woman would cease to have a job!

AIDS has effected great cultural change. In Africa, if a parent, or parents, died then the extended family would take over care of the children, but the AIDS epidemic has been so great in some parts of Africa that that the cultural norm has been breaking down. In Kenya, for example, for a time there were up to 700 people per day dying from AIDS.

In this situation those old 'norms' break down and the culture changes; so where there were once no orphanages because the family was extended and could cope there are now large orphanages, and many children also living on the street with no one responsible for them.

Technology also affects change. We have seen that in the UK: washing machines, dishwashers, cars, aeroplanes and, of late, mobile phones, fax machines, computers and the www all cause huge changes to take place in the culture.

Who could have imagined hoards of school children leaving school at 3.30pm chatting to their friends on a mobile phone, or the ability to talk on MSN around the world, or now to SKYPE to the other side of the world with a camera affixed, for free? These technologies change our culture. They change our perceptions, expectations, actions and culture.

I have already said that the media has a powerful effect on a culture and changes it. The domination of Hollywood and Bollywood has world-wide reach and creates massive changes in the world culture. The studios also increase, and create, massive expectations and often massive disappointments when, what is held out as 'normal' life, or reality, cannot be achieved by the majority of people. There are those who are very aware of the power of these cultural models and some would use them for good, some for evil. The world of advertising is very powerful. It always makes me laugh when advertisers on television try to tell us that they are not affecting the way we live or the value system in our culture. If that is the case why do they pay such large sums of money for those advertising slots?

Language changes, moulds and makes culture as well. I used to think it was a bit silly to change words in English simply to be the politically correct: manhole to 'person entrance'; chairman to 'chairperson'. I changed my mind. Words are powerful and if we use the wrong ones in the wrong way they have an effect on us. Change them and they can change our thinking and, eventually, the culture.

Let me tell you a story—one that I don't really understand but was able to observe. I was standing outside a meeting in Paris talking to a friend, an American lady, but quite a linguist; I think she speaks about nine languages. We had just finished a meeting with a Tamil group. I don't speak Tamil and my French is very bad, so I was sticking to English. My Tamil friends, on the other hand, are very multi-lingual. This group spoke Tamil, French and English fluently. My American friend asked if I wanted to see something interesting. I did, so she advised me to watch and I would see something strange. All the young Tamil teenagers were chatting in the Tamil language. Tamil culture is what I call a very, very, 'non touchy' culture. You don't even shake hands; you say 'hello' by putting your own hands together with a slight bow to say hello, and, boy-oh-boy, you never touch a person of the opposite sex, particularly if you are in your teens. I observed that the conversation was going on in a very Tamil way. Lots of words, bobbing and hand and head movements, but certainly no touching, oh dear no!

My friend then approached the group to join in the conversation.

I leaned against a tree on that Paris street and watched as my friend spoke some Tamil (though, the Tamils said, with very bad grammar). As the conversation continued in Tamil, now including my friend, the Tamil cultural protocols continued. Then, suddenly, my friend changed language and began to speak French. I guess because she was there, and because to this group of teenagers one language is as easy as another, they all began to speak French, but then it hit me … not only had the language of words and sounds changed but the language of the body also changed, this non touchy group now became very touchy French people.

All of a sudden they were touching each others hands and arms and kissing on the cheek as they prepared to leave in very French fashion. Gone where all the non touchy ways and now they seemed to be very un-circumspect; now they where very un-Tamil; now they where French and just a few words had changed the cultural actions.

I don't fully understand what happened, but I saw it!

Laws effect changes in culture. As the divorce laws have become easier in Britain divorce has increased. That has put cultural pressure on families. 100, or even 60, years ago there was extended family in the UK. Usually families lived close to each other, often in the same streets, so if you had a bad father or mother at least your cousin might have a good one, so you got to see a range of expressions of family.

Now we have broken that extended family down into small units with Dad, Mum and two children, or what I call the mini family, moving away from the extended family. Then, with divorce on the increase we have moved to the micro family: single parent and child. This has increased pressure on housing; creating shortages. It also means that fathers don't really know how to be fathers, they haven't ever seen it demonstrated, and so we have many of the cultural problems that we see in our country. Fathers don't naturally know how to act; they are often drawing from their own childhood experience of what they have seen. If they haven't seen much, or anything at all, of their own fathers, why would we assume that the knowledge is there?

One thing is sure: if we want to change a culture, any culture—that of a country, a public service, a company, a charity, or a church—the only way we can change it is by engaging with it. It would help us to know, of course, what it is and what we want to change. That will all come back to the need for us to define our own basic value system, for that also will have a powerful affect on our culture.

CHAPTER SIX

CULTURE AND THE CHANGE FACTOR

As has been said a few times already change in culture is happening all the time. The thing is, though, much of cultural change had taken place over many hundreds of years. Change that is gradual can usually be dealt with. It isn't scary and, indeed, many times we are not aware of the changes taking place as they are so gradual.

In history that would not always have been the case. Such things as huge movements of people because of war, famine and drought would have affected areas where those people ended up and could have caused large cultural shifts.

Other big shifts in culture would have been things like the Irish potato famine, the invention of the spinning Jenny in the textile industry and the whole change caused by the industrial revolution in the West. Changing a culture of cottage industry into centralised factory work must have had huge cultural implications.

Change can be painful. We often want to resist change which is out of the ordinary person's control, such as industrial change or information technology advancements.

So, after World War Two, many returning soldiers wanted to go back to the pre-war status quo, i.e. wife stay home, and husband goes out to work. The problem was that many of the ladies had experienced working, and for them there were great benefits in it. The increased human interaction and the acquisition of their own disposable income offered a freedom that they had not perceived was possible before the war; so most of them did not want to go back to the previous status quo. The genie was out of the bottle! The culture had changed and the ladies liked it!

The industrial revolution created change of a massive nature. From the rural cottage industries now came the large manufacturing industries such as cotton, clothing, coal, iron and steel manufacturing on a large basis. Mechanisation led to the assembly line of the car manufacturer and even the assembly line of the chocolate makers! This meant that workers were needed in greater numbers and the closer they were to the factories that produced the goods the more efficient it was for the producer; therefore cheap housing was often erected in close proximity to the factory. As wages were a little better than in the countryside there was a migration of workers into the city; the pull of urbanisation. For large amounts of people this pull has continued and is still going on. We now see massive urbanisation across the whole world. This urbanisation has caused huge change, not just in work and family but changing a whole cultural tradition that had lasted hundreds of years.

Just for your interest I have detailed below the changes, and the continual pull, of urbanisations beginning with the 1950s:

1950.
1. NEW YORK 12.3 MILLION
2. LONDON 8.7 MILLION
3. TOKYO 6.7. MILLION
4. PARIS 5.4 MILLION
5. SHANGHAI 5.3 MILLION
6. BUENOS AIRES 5.1 MILLION
7. CHICAGO 4.9. MILLION
8. MOSCOW 4.8 MILLION
9. CALCUTTA 4.4. MILLION
10. LOS ANGELES 4 MILLION

And then we move on to the year 2000.

2000.
1. MEXICO CITY 25.6 MILLION
2. SAO PAULO 22.1 MILLION
3. TOKYO 19.1 MILLION
4. SHANGHAI 17 MILLION
5. NEW YORK 15.7 MILLION
6. CALCUTTA 15.7 MILLION
7. MUMBAI 15.4 MILLION
8. BEIJING 14 MILLION
9. JAKARTA 13.7 MILLION
10. LOS ANGELES 13.9 MILLION

And then on to the current day:

City	Population	Country
1. TOKYO	35,197,000	JAPAN
2. MEXICO CITY	19,411,000	MEXICO
3. NEW YORK CITY-NEWARK	18,718,000	UNITED STATES
4. SÃO PAULO	18,333,000	BRAZIL
5. MUMBAI	18,196,000	INDIA
6. GREATER CAIRO	17,856,000	EGYPT
7. DELHI	15,048,000	INDIA
8. SHANGHAI	14,503,000	PEOPLE'S REPUBLIC OF CHINA
9. KOLKATA	14,277,000	INDIA
10. JAKARTA (JABODETABEK)	13,215,000	INDONESIA

Most of us cope with change in small doses; problems occur when we go through rapid cultural changes that make us feel insecure. We lose our anchor points; we feel out of control; we get confused, particularly as we grow older. So, witness the monetary change in the UK from the imperial system (based around multiples of 12) to a decimalisation process. Many still have not got to grips with it and it will take a completely new generation before total acceptance.

Then, consider the communication change of our current era: Internet, Fax machines, Mobile Phone—a whole plethora of change that for the new generation is just fine; but watch what happened to older generations. I bought my wife an old fashioned phone; one with a dial on; the kind you put your finger in and move it around to the required number or letter. One 14 year old said, "But what is it?" "A phone" I replied. "But it doesn't have any buttons on, how are you supposed to make a call with it?" she asked. I demonstrated how to use the phone, to which she responded "I couldn't do that, I would break my nails!"

The same young lady asked me what TV I watched when I was 14 years old. It was hard to explain that TV wasn't really around. Radio was still a fascination and TV did not hit until around 1953. "So what on earth did you do?" she asked. "Well, I read books," I replied. "You did what?" came the incredulous response!

Technology, along with all sorts of other things, has the power to change culture. It changes the way we live, and therefore the way we think. It may even make us challenge our value system, which means that to have a value system that lasts we must be sure where it comes from. Is it just that which is passed on from neighbourhood, to neighbourhood, tribe to tribe, family to family, or is the basis for our value system more time tested and from a higher source?

CHAPTER SEVEN

CULTURE AND THE ROLE OF WOMEN

Many young people, and particularly many young ladies who live in the West, do not really understand the changes that have taken place in the last 100 years. Sadly, some young people are not particularly interested in history and what has happened to form our culture and how we got here; but it does us good to understand how we have arrived at where we are. Without that knowledge there are missing links to our actions and our way of life.

We ought to learn from history; we ought not to make the mistakes of history. The problem is that we do not learn from history and we make the same mistakes over and over again. If we don't even take the trouble to understand it a little then there is something really missing in our persona.

In this chapter we are going to look at the role of women in culture. From the latter half of the last century right up to the present day women's perspectives (particularly in the Western world) have gone through massive change in areas such as work, child rearing, use of money and the law, plus many other areas that we would want to, and ought to, consider.

One should not simply, however, consider women's roles solely in your own country. Please try and think about what women do in other countries, particularly in third world countries.

Look at their choices in terms of marriage, work and education. Consider both their economic well being and their economic contribution to the family and the nation as a whole. Ask yourself how influential they are in these areas and what would need—if anything to allow them to be more or less so?

Historically, what was it that brought about change for women in the UK; and there have been huge changes? One of the major things that have effected these changes was the last World War. What happened in the UK was that men went off to fight; huge numbers of them! That left the UK factories short on manpower; and that manpower was necessary for the war effort. It was needed to produce munitions, transport, aeroplanes as well as keeping the country more or less running; so the employers of manpower turned to women power.

Up until this time women had been expected to be homemakers. Even companies like Cadburys chocolate—which had a great justice perspective being one of the first companies to introduce workers representatives to their board and seeking to give good housing to its employees hence 'Bourneville a factory in a garden'—even they went with the culture of the time and assumed that if a female employee got married she would no longer be working. That was the culturally accepted norm. Can you see how things have changed?

Indeed, Cadburys had a tradition of presenting a young lady who announced her marriage with a wedding present of a Bible, a Carnation, and of course her cards, P45 in today's UK parlance. It really was not that long ago and can still be remembered by many people today.

So, for a married woman to go out to work was strange indeed until those war years. You get a glimpse of the culture that was as you look at the early TV advertisements for domestic appliances. Advertisements from the early 1950s all show women with vacuum cleaners, washing machines and irons that where about to change their life! They could still be at home, but would be able to sit down and do nothing as the machines would do the work! I am not sure what they thought would be done in this wonderful women's world of leisure.

The great shock for men returning from the war to their spouses and would be wives was to discover that the ladies where not for returning to a previous paradigm. They liked going out to work; they liked the socialising of the work place; they liked the freedom that the extra money gave them; they wanted a new world and that caused upheavals; and is still causing them today. Why do I say today? Well, check out how many times you hear a news item of the fact that women have still not achieved salary parity in this or that job; check out how many surveys discuss the role of a woman in a home, particularly where there is a couple that both have full time jobs. Who is it that does the major part of the work in a house or with children? Our historical perspectives are not that easy to shake off. Sure, there is more equality, but the historical cultural perspective is still there and is quite strong, even amongst new generations.

The cultural role of women in the world is a particularly important one; very important when we want to bring about change!

It is well acknowledged that where woman are given the opportunity to earn or to develop business this has the effect of huge cultural shifts, for when women are earning then the children are sent to school, better fed better, educated better and looked after and so change for a nation begins to take place.

Think about the things that have changed for women in the West, though sadly not throughout the world as a whole. Things like the vote[vii], lades in the UK could only do that post 1918 Swiss women not until 1971[viii], and that is in the 'enlightened' west. Also, the right to work, water on tap, cooking appliances, the expectation that men might cook and clean too! It was only just over a 130 years ago that women in the UK who where married actually had no right even to the money they earned themselves. That was the property of the husband as was she herself; as were any children from the marriage[ix]. The wife owned nothing and was herself owned by her husband!

I love to ask newcomers to the UK what the biggest difference is that they have noted. A young lady who had just arrived from a small village in Africa retorted to this "You people never cook!" I, of course, said "that's not true, of course we cook!" to which she replied, "No you don't, you put it in that machine, it goes 'ping' and you have a meal". She had never been in contact with a microwave until then. I asked her what she meant by cooking a meal. "Well ..." she said, "That's almost a day's work! I have to walk to the river to get water; which is a long way. Then I have to take another long walk to find firewood ... then, if it is to be chicken, I have to catch a chicken, chop of its head and then pluck and clean it. Only then am I ready to cook it along with some meal. That is a very long, long job!" I understood!

All of these 'business' activities have cultural effects that when you change you make a major difference that affects the culture as a whole. I have seen the effects in other countries of the introduction of a water tank so people did not have to spend hours walking for water; I watched the huge effect in South Africa of the introduction of television; I have seen first hand the benefits of mobile phones to the small-holding African farmer as he can check, from his village, the price of maize selling in places like Nairobi. Technology changes things, but change the life of a woman and you will have an even more powerful effect on the culture at large. Look at what has happened in the West ... and in many other countries, it's not clever new technology that is needed but simply to make clean water more readily available, not even, necessarily piped in. A plastic water tank that will collect rain water will change a lot. Do you want to change a culture, look hard at the role of women within that society and see how it can be improved!

CHAPTER EIGHT
HOW URBANIZATION CHANGES CULTURE

Some years ago I was on one of my very regular visits to Sri Lanka. On this occasion I was invited to go right up to the North East to a place called Trincomalee. It was a long train journey from Colombo the capital, taking us through the jungle in some places; and at a time of quite high tension as fighting had begun again in the North. Our train stopped just before we entered the jungle and soldiers with rifles got on the train and were posted at every window and door of the train. I looked out at the jungle and pondered their role, hoping they had better eye-sight than I had because I couldn't see past the first line of trees!

Accompanying me on the journey were leaders from Colombo churches and a whole crowd of Colombo young people, mostly in their teens and many of whom had not been to this part of their own country always having lived in the capital.

On arrival at our destination, having passed the tight security at the railway station with bag and personal searches, we moved off down the main street of Trincomalee.

It was a busy day with lots of people around, and, of course, many of them stared at this strange white man in their midst—me, that is! That didn't surprise me as not many foreign visitors were going there at that time. I also noticed something else about the curiosity of the local people. They paid as much, if not more attention to the strange crowd of young Tamils from Colombo. These youngsters, whilst speaking the language, which I don't, and being part of the country, which I am not, nevertheless stood out like a sore thumb in this small town. I watched as they walked down the main street with interest.

The way they walked was different to the locals. Their talk was kind of different too; perhaps a bit louder; although that did not seem to be just because they were teenagers as there were teenagers watching. The differences extended to all sort of things: dress, talk, walk, type of conversation; what I was observing was the change brought about by urbanisation.

Currently, in North London, I work with refugees and asylum seekers from all over the world. We have people coming for our help from Ethiopia, Kosovo, Vietnam, China, Iraq, Iran, Congo, Rwanda, and on and on. We often meet these people when they first come to the UK and I am always amused at how quickly they absorb the London look, dress, conversation, mobile phones, and the whole paraphernalia of urbanisation gets added so quickly. One young man told me that before he had been driven out of his country and ran to the UK for his life, he had been a shepherd all his life; it was the only thing he knew. Now it was … 'how do I use this computer?' … 'Where can I get a mobile phone?' … 'How do I talk and look?' The city moulds us and makes us and can certainly challenge and change our original cultural actions and perspectives.

The city changes us because there are often so many different people and ideas and cultures all rubbing together. London speaks hundreds of languages; it eats food from around the world; its entertainment is multi-ethnic, every religion and philosophy is represented. You would really have to be a very practised hermit to not be affected by the clatter and noise and variety of the city. Some people might hate that. I like it! I like being challenged by others' thinking; the fact that they are outside of my box. Their experiences are different; their food is different. I want to be impacted by it; I don't want to live in a box. I want to understand what makes others tick, why they think the way they do, and I want to be constantly checking that my value statement is good, and right. I want to be on solid ground. I am sure I am, and for that reason I am not afraid of the city.

The fact is, as you should see from the statistics, that urbanisation is a huge reality in our world. All over the world more and more of us live in large cities. We need to understand them, we need to know them, and we need a value system that will enable us to be secure in them. The reality is that urbanisation is changing everything, including what we thought was our culture, that is, if we ever did think about it.

I have always been amused that Christians tend to emphasise the country. How often do you see pictures of lambs skipping on Christian pamphlets and calendars, or supposedly idyllic country scenes: flowers, fields, crows flying and the like?

When did you ever see a picture of a city and urban sprawl? I reckon very rarely! It's seen, it seems to me, that Christians regard cities as somehow evil. I am sure there is evil in them, and I think the countryside has too; however my reading of the Bible gives me the impression that God quite likes cities. There is a lot more mention of them than some people would give credit to. In fact ultimately, it seems from my reading of the Bible, God promises us a city.

Cities can be a place of security and safety; they certainly can be a place of innovation and change. Yes, they develop their own culture but that is not necessarily bad. They are places of great commerce and exchange both in terms of goods and services and in term of ideas and often progression. Long live the city, I say, and I will live with the pressure on my given culture, how about you?

CHAPTER NINE

THE IMPORTANCE OF META-NARRATIVE

What is a meta-narrative? Many of you reading this will not know; even though most of you will have one. Simply put, a meta-narrative means the big picture. Our meta-narrative is very powerful within our understanding of a cultural perspective, because it will colour everything we think and are.

Most cultures, even in our Post Modern world, (Post Modernism we will look at later) use a meta-narrative to understand who they are and where they are in the world in which they live. We do that to give us position; to understand where to go and why.

If you are a Communist, Muslim, Christian, or Hindu you will have a meta-narrative. It really means that you have a world view. That world view, or big picture, will help you navigate the world and will, to a great extent, impact on your cultural views. Your world view will have a start, (somehow, somewhere, that's where it began), it will have a middle, (that is somewhere that you are at the moment) and it will have an end (where we go or end up; the ultimate aim). You will interpret the world around you according to your own world view. It will help you to make sense of the world in which you live.

So for many of us a meta-narrative is important. We use it even though we didn't know that we were. There will, however, be a clash from those in our 'new world' who do not hold a meta-narrative world view. Those who hold a post modern view will not use the same kind of logic to arrive at a conclusion as those who have a meta-narrative will.

Often it amuses me when people talk about working through things without prejudice; objectively; as if they have a clean sheet. As if you can! How do we? How can we get outside of ourselves?

Even when we are not conscious of that meta-narrative we are still working within the confines of it. That does not mean we cannot be caused to check our own world view and value system when we come up against those who have a different view.

What about those that do not hold a meta-narrative world view? What do I mean by that? Well, increasingly in the West we find many who hold a post modern world view, and that world view works in a very different way; impacting on all of our cultures.

So how does a post modern world view work, as opposed to a meta-narrative world view?

Currently, in our world, we have young people who I would call people with a post modern world view. Much like those who have a meta-narrative it is a label that often they would not recognise. Much like those who hold a meta-narrative view it is just a way of living and often is not well thought through. So let me try and define what I think a post modern world view looks like.

This world view is not interested in beginnings and endings, history or future; it is very interested in the present, the now. What is happening now; is it good or is it bad? The experience of the moment is all important. This lifestyle allows people to hold views that, when you apply modernist logic to them, don't hold water! They are totally opposed to each other! They don't meet or match, but because experience is everything that does not matter. Discussion about right or wrong becomes almost irrelevant as it depends on the now and on how you feel at the present moment!

This view means that value systems are on a sliding scale so what is right today might be wrong tomorrow depending on what is happening. What you thought was good one day becomes bad another because the situation has changed.

Not everything in this world view is negative. The post modernist is very interested in spiritual things, but the negative of that is that spirituality is a little like a sweet shop's pick and mix! The post modernist loves stories, but is not particularly interested in joining the stories together to make a big picture, so the stories become interesting as a momentary thing but are like graded pearls on a necklace that has had the string broken.

Often, the post modernist has a concern about justice but again this becomes fragmented as it hits the experience spot and the focus is changed by a new day's experience.

We probably need to ask what the pressures are that have created this new post modern generation; the generation that some journalists call generation 'X'.

Our world has gone through huge change in the last 50 years; change that has been greater and faster than at any other time in history: massive innovations via technology—computers, faxes, mobile phones, satellites, digital T.V., space rockets … to name just a few.

Along with that massive change has come other things; things like the loss of absolutes. Post modernists cannot understand or believe in an absolute truth; it doesn't exist!

If there is no absolute then it follows that there is no moral base, and if there is no moral base then we have to have situation ethics—so what is happening at the moment sets the agenda, both moral and otherwise.

Whilst there is a revival in the interest of spirituality, at least in the UK, nevertheless there has also been a loss of spirituality; the kind of spirituality that holds a meta-narrative—a big picture world view. Recently post modernism has moved to a loss in faith in science, this is, in part, due to such things as mad cow disease, and the earlier thalidomide debacle.

All these things cause a loss of traditions. Now there are some traditions we might want to lose, but when we lose lots of them quickly it destabilises us and creates a neurosis in our culture, and all these things have also combined to develop what I am calling our post modern society.

Post-modernism has strength in that it dares to experiment, that's one of those positive things. It is a creative society in that it thinks in colours and pictures, but that creativity lacks a touchstone of morality or the moral line tied to absolutes that guide experimentation. This provides an exciting but dangerous society to live in. If our culture is to be turned around for the better we had better understand the historical perspective that tells us how we have got here and where we should set course to go; otherwise we are heading not only for the shipwreck of culture but for the crash of our total humanity, and its intrinsic worth.

CHAPTER TEN
OUR PRESUPPOSITIONS

I have said this before, but let me say it again. It is to me an amazing fact that people often think they are being objective and working on some thought with a clean sheet, totally disbelieving that they have their own meta-narrative, and denying even more strongly that their presuppositions persuade and colour the results before they are obtained.

All of us have presuppositions, yet most of the time we are not even aware of that fact. The fact is we are using our presuppositions all the time, analyzing the world around us.

We come to conclusions, we think, on the basis of facts. The problem is that none of us can ever really be totally objective.

Our presuppositions colour everything. We look at the facts and then come to a conclusion based on our presuppositions. We should be aware that with a different cultural base, a different set of presuppositions, a different meta-narrative programmed into us we would, when we look at the same set of facts, quite likely end up with a different conclusion.

In the course complementing this book we try some fun things like the GODISNOWHERE exercise. Now of course that is not scientific or really objective, but I think it illustrates a point. If our presupposition was that God does not exist then we are likely to read God is nowhere; whereas if our presupposition is that there is a God then maybe we would read the same set of letters as God is now here. Of course this does not prove anything except that we see things differently and therefore come to a different answer.

It is too simple to say that our conclusions on the above are because of our presuppositions; however it would do us good to ask ourselves, methinks the question why it is, when two people look at the same thing, they come to different answers. Now, if you have two people from totally different cultural backgrounds, how different will the answers be to a given same set of situations? Let us recognise that others come to a different conclusion even though they are looking at the same scenarios from the same angle.

In terms of our presuppositions we need to begin to examine the things that we did not necessarily know were there: our perceptions. We need to question our presuppositions, which ones we have, where they come from and how family, culture, schooling and personal history has programmed those presuppositions into me.

Am I saying that we can never be objective? Well, I am saying that it is very hard to do. However, if we start to examine our presuppositions, which often we do not even think about, then we could be on the way to arriving at better conclusions as we look at life. We need to also recognise that some of our presuppositions may turn out to be correct. And, conversely, we should also be willing to discover that our presuppositions may turn out to be totally wrong and need to be ditched.

Some people never examine their presuppositions. For me, going to college where I had to mix with many different nationalities caused me to examine my presuppositions. It was sometimes a painful experience as I was forced to question why I believed certain things and where these views came from. Often, of course, it was family generated, sometimes culturally given, sometimes from school and growing up with a certain set of peers. I felt it was a little like peeling an onion; asking where did this come from; it may have been given to me, but is it correct? I found that, for some things, I was putting them on one side as I found they no longer fitted with lots of other things that were now important. For other things I was able to say 'this is a solid gold value—let me really hold on to it'.

Naturally, as I grew up in a time when meta-narratives were given I did not have to struggle with a post modern view.

My meta-narrative therefore did not give me permission in myself to hold two separate and contradictory views, which I often find people, particularly young people, can do these days.

So what is my plea here in this chapter? Well, that we think about and examine our own presuppositions; that we ask where they came from; ask what is it that is a really positive value system to live by; ask whether there is, indeed, a meta-narrative that makes sense of the world. There are those who would have us subscribe to the fact that the world is just an accident, there is no design; there is no purpose; there is no future; there is no God. There is just the accident of now. If you can subscribe to that view of life, that will produce, in you, a good post modern world view. I don't believe it and don't want to live like it.

I want a view of life that gives a valuable value system; a purpose to be here; a purpose to life, to the world, life with a future. You might say well that is the product of your presuppositions, which are the result of your upbringing. Well, so be it!

CHAPTER ELEVEN
THE CLASH OF CULTURES

One of the main reasons for writing this book was because of my observations concerning cultural clashes. Working, as I do, within the field of counselling and foster care I became very aware of how our presuppositions and meta-narratives colour our expectations. I also noted how it was that, when our expectations, no matter how unreasonable they may be, are disappointed it often makes us cross and angry, never mind extremely disappointed.

In chapter 2 I mentioned a lady who was in one of my training programmes who, after my lecture, told the group that she was going back to continue working with a young Ghanaian lad who she had previously decided she would give up on. The reason she gave for giving up? Well, he looked away when talking with her.

Her culture suggested to her that he was rude and shifty while, from his cultural perspective he was actually being polite and showing her respect. In Ghanaian culture you don't make eye contact to people older than yourself unless you want to be rude!

I am often surprised how rude we can be when we do not understand. Usually our approach is based on ignorance. How often have I heard people insult each others food tastes, as though the cooking from their culture is the only kind to eat!

Cultural expressions via clothes are another source of conflict and clash. Working, as I do, with churches in many countries it is interesting that when I am in non-western countries clothing is often discussed. I find that there is often conflict in this area and intolerance by all concerned; definitely a recipe for a clash.

Another major culture clash comes between age groups as they seek to decide what is culturally acceptable. Again, speaking from my foster care experience, I found that foster carers had an expectation of young people based on their own upbringing and culturally accepted norms which often clashed with the people they where looking after. There was, and often is, a biased assumption, not thought through, that 'my culture is right, and therefore my way of doing, acting, thinking and arriving at a conclusion must also be right'. Often we are not willing to allow the fact that someone's way of doing or thinking is not necessarily wrong just because it is different from ours. Maybe it's just that—different! This problem of clash often comes between age groups and their various expectations.

I do not subscribe to the view that seems to be sometimes lifted high in the medium of TV documentaries and other modern media and is in danger of entering the annals of political correctness and normality. This is the idea that if it comes from our culture it must be the right thing to hold on to. I think that is a totally wrong headed idea, just plain daft, but to counter it we need something else in which to place our trust, or to put it another way—some way of getting a cultural check.

So, where do we get a cultural check from? I believe we need to get it from our value system, but that begs the question: who sets the value system? Is it to be governed by the wider culture, situational ethics, a friend's opinion or what? As a Christian, and a follower of Christ, I would want my own personal value system to be checked against the touchstone of what He thinks and the way He would expect me to work and the culture norms that He would expect me to adopt. Someone said that there is no such thing as a 'Christian Culture', and to a certain extent I understand the thinking behind that statement. However, it must also be true to say that a basic value system will affect a wider cultural perspective. It should also be possible to look at a wider culture, to seek to ascertain what the underlying principals of this culture are; what is the value system that has influenced its establishment, are they values of Justice, Righteousness, Peace etc., do they put a high value on humanity and its dignity, or are some humans regarded as somehow lesser than others. This may be something that we should really think about and look at on the macro scale.

So, if we want to avoid cultural clashes it needs to start with our own personal understanding and education.

That may not, of course, avoid the clash altogether; for even when we have understood another's culture we may find the underlying value system unacceptable. One example for me would be the following story:

I had invited a local Canadian Pastor to meet with me over a cup of coffee. This was in London and he told me he was pastoring a local Kurdish church. He explained to me that he was currently finding it difficult to deal with some of the arising pastoral issues.

"Like what?" I asked.

"Well," he went on "it's a cultural problem. The men are beating their wives too much because there is not the control that there would be in their homeland."

I responded with, "I don't quite understand what you mean when you say they are beating their wives 'too much'. Are you saying that beating them some is acceptable to you?"

"Well, of course," he replied. "That is part of their culture, but when they beat them too much they could end up killing them."

I said, "Well, personally I cannot accept the fact that any beating should be acceptable!"

He got very cross with me, saying that I obviously had no understanding of culture, and wouldn't even stop to finish his coffee!

I still have that same problem, and do not think that that clash could have been avoided. My value system leads me to strongly oppose such thinking coming from a culture or not!

CHAPTER TWELVE

COMPANY CULTURES

When thinking of cultures we can of course get stuck in the tribal, local area, national frame, and think only of cultures in those terms, but of course that would be very limiting. We are becoming aware of the way in which our lives are affected by the culture of companies. We even use the phrase 'company man'—in other words someone who is not only loyal to the company but understands the company rules, written or otherwise—and usually the unwritten are more powerful.

In the UK I believe that there has been an attempt to change various cultures, such as the culture in the National Health Service and the Culture in the Royal Mail. I don't pretend to know what those cultures are but I am sure that just injecting money into a project will not always change things in the way that you expect because not only are you dealing with performance quotas and business targets; you are dealing with a culture of work and expectation of how work is done over a long period. 'Culture' is often the most difficult area to change in any business or organisation.

Then we should not forget that in most countries there are, what I call, sub-cultures. That probably is the wrong term, for in reality they really are 'their own culture'. So, we have a culture, for example, amongst the deaf community in the UK and another amongst the blind community also. As I have said before, I have worked for many years in the area of foster care. What often amazes me is how, amongst foster children, there is a culture. Often in an area the foster children know each other, although perhaps that should not be so surprising as often events are organised for them and they get to meet their peers.

That has knock-on implications, both useful and difficult. Often the children know the system better than their carers; they have a cultural perspective about how things work or don't work and some of those perspectives are incorrect or, from my point of view, culturally wrong. That cultural perspective can send wrong information, and that information gets picked up by others such as teachers, police, and government agencies and they act on their preconceptions, which are also wrong. So, preconceptions people may have will be, such as: 'all foster children are in care because they are difficult children' which is wrong. It may be a much more complex situation which has more to do with the parent's situation—maybe the mother is ill and the father has had to keep working!

The statistics show that foster children generally leave school without any qualifications, but I wonder whether that is really because they are not as bright. I think, instead, is that we label, and then, rather than help these young people fulfil their potential, wait for the outcome that fits our wrong labelling. It's a bit like if you are expecting a problem you will find one.

Our perspectives do count, like the rhyme says: 'Two men looked out of prison bars, the one saw mud the other saw stars! Which view would you be looking upon? I guess mud could be quite depressing to regard all day; and maybe the stars inspiring. A simple change in viewing angle, a change in perspective, could make all the difference.

In some ways we can be helped to understand how difficult it is (difficult, not impossible) to change culture when we look at culture on the smaller scale—the culture of our office; the culture of the school or college we go to; the culture of the company that we run or work in. How did that culture come about? Where did it start? From who, or from where, did the ideas come from—both the wrong ideas and the right ideas? How can we change the wrong ones? What levers do we need to push and pull; what buttons we can press?

In conclusion, I hope that this book has helped you to think. Think about your culture; think about where it came from, why you are who and what you are. Is it good? Is it not so good? Are there things that should be changed? How can I change them? What is my value system? Where did that value system come from? What is my thinking like? What feeds my thinking? Are there ways that I should change that to start with? If so, what should I use to change my thinking? Our thinking is that if the Bible is correct (and I believe it to be so), then it is our thoughts that mould us and make us (*as we think in our hearts so we are—Proverbs 23: 7)*; for our thinking is that which generates the way we act.

So … happy thinking and let's change our cultures for the better!

References

i   Bible references

ii   PEPA Art group Rainbow church North London

iii   Christian Overman 'Things that shape our thinking'

iv   Maslow's pyramid of needs

v   Dr Patrick Dixon M.D.//leighbureau.com

vi   Financial Times Monday October 31st 2005

vii   Historical records. Before 1918 only men were allowed to vote. Women aged 30 or over gained the right to vote in 1918—the same year that women were first able to be MPs—but it was not until 1928 that the voting age for women was lowered to 21 (the same age as for men at that time).

viii   **1971: Swiss women get the vote Source BBC** Although Swiss women can now vote in most regional and national elections; they continue to face discrimination under Swiss law. At home, men retain control of their wives' property and capital, and the husband has the right to decide where he and his wife will reside.

ix   In 1870, women were allowed to keep money they had earned. Source History learning.

TRAINERS NOTES FILE

BARNABAS TRAINING CULTURE AT DIPLOMA LEVEL

Barnabas Training International

TRAINING COURSE ON THE SUBJECT OF CULTURE
THIS COURSE WILL HAVE A MINIMUM OF 35 HOURS CONTACT TIME PLUS SOME 25 HOURS OF HOME WORK STUDY TIME.

TRAINING COURSE ON THE SUBJECT OF CULTURE
THIS COURSE WILL HAVE A MINIMUM OF 35 HOURS CONTACT TIME PLUS SOME 25 HOURS OF HOME WORK STUDY TIME.

BARNABAS TRAINING INTERNATIONAL

INDEX FOR CULTURAL COURSE

1. WHAT IS CULTURE? 58
2. DEFINITIONS 61
3. THE BASE PILLARS OF CULTURE 62
4. WHY IS KNOWING ABOUT CULTURE IMPORTANT? 66
5. HOW CULTURES ARE FORMED 71
6. DEFINING A CULTURE 74
7. LANGUAGE AND CULTURE 76
8. CULTURE AND THE CHANGE FACTOR 78
9. CULTURAL CHANGE IN OUR WORLD 79
10. CULTURE AND THE ROLE OF WOMEN 82
11. HOW URBANISATION CHANGES CULTURE 83
12. THE IMPORTANCE OF META-NARRATIVE 84
13. OUR PRESUPPOSITIONS!!! 86
14. OBSERVABLE CHANGE THAT IS CURRENTLY PUTTING PRESSURE ON OUR CULTURE AND CHANGING IT 88
15. SUB CULTURES AND SPECIAL CULTURES 90
16. THE DOMINATING OR DOMINANT CULTURE 93

17. WHAT ARE THE PRESSURES AND BENEFITS OF
 CULTURE ON FAMILY 95
18. SPECIAL GUEST LECTURE FROM 'THROUGH THE ROOF'—
 PEOPLE WITH DISABILITIES AND THEIR CULTURE 97
19. THE CLASH OF CULTURES 98
20. COURSE END/SUMMARY/ PRESENTATION OF
 COMPLETION CERTIFICATES 99

> TRAINING COURSE ON THE SUBJECT OF CULTURE
> THIS COURSE WILL HAVE A MINIMUM OF 35 HOURS CONTACT
> TIME PLUS SOME 25 HOURS OF HOME WORK STUDY TIME.

The Purpose of the Course

The purpose of the course is not to discover right and wrong about culture, but to understand, first of all, ourselves. What expectations have we taken on board as a result of our culture? Do we even think about our own culture and what it is? If we live in a fairly mono-cultural area, or surround ourselves with people who are 'very much like us', then we probably don't even think about the subject. It would not be wrong to say things like there are similarities in English people who live in the North of England and English people who live in the South, but that would be too simplistic a conclusion. We need better understanding than that. If we are using this course to inform us because we are a counsellor then it becomes very important. Peoples' cultures make them arrive at different answers from the same set of perspectives. We must be careful, however, as we go through the training set out by this course not to become complacent in terms of acceptance of cultural norms as being ok, just because they are culturally accepted. For example, just because it is a culturally accepted thing for men to beat their wives in a particular culture, does that mean that it is right and we should just go along with the culture? After all, it's their culture and we shouldn't interfere with that should we?

Expected Out-Come of the Course

At the end of this course the student should understand

- o   Where Culture comes from
- o   How Culture is formed
- o   How culture is changed
- o   Be aware of other cultures
- o   Be willing to see things from another perspective by understanding another's preconceptions

They should realise how our

- Ideas
- Thinking and

- Presuppositions all affect our
- Conclusions

The course will be assessed for student understanding
By essays
By film reports
By book reports

By analytical report on a set subject within the course

EXTRA PRELIMINARY INFORMATION:-

1. There is a varying amount of POWERPOINT presentations for use during this course. Obviously the trainer can mix or match, or can use material added to the presentation. We have included POWERPOINT No.11 which covers more or less the whole essence of the course. This could be used as a revision, or not used at all, depending on the trainer's approach.

2. We have obtained the use of HSBC bank advertising DVD for use by the course. As you may know the HSBC bank uses the differences in culture to emphasise the fact that it is the 'World's Local Bank'. It would be good to use this either in the course or as an introduction to the course. We are grateful to the bank for allowing us to use their material.

3. We have invited the students and trainers to use both films and books to understand this course better, and we would recommend the trainers to encourage students to look at both sources for their material and essay writing.

4. We will, from time to time, add books and films to the course as we continue to review the material. Please advise us of material that you believe would be relevant.

Trainers Notes

1. WHAT IS CULTURE?

> For this first part of the course the trainer needs to allow a good hour. The lecture should take account of the fact that many people actually do not think about culture, particularly if they live in an area where people around them are very much like themselves. This will not be true in a large major conurbation where people are surrounded by a multi-racial, multi-cultural multi-ethnic and multi-religious community. There people often can be very aware of differences in culture, but even then they may not think of the pressures and moulders that make a culture; and it is those things that the trainer needs to be trying to 'dig' out of students on this course. As well as lecture material, it would be good to use 'quick think' and flip chart answers to help the group focus on the material of what, where and how?

- **What is Culture?**
- **Where does it come from?**
- **What makes it?**

<u>It is the effect of family and pressures by</u>
- Politics/Religion
- Education
- Art/Media
- Economics

What are the easy things to spot that demonstrate differences in culture?

<u>Differences in Cultures that are obvious</u>
Things like:-
- Food
- Greetings
- Dress
- Language

The four pillars of culture
- Business/economics
- Education/family
- Media/entertainment/advertising
- Politics/government/religion

Are the four pillars on which all culture rests

Culture is not static
- It is constantly changing, though sometimes we are not aware of that fact
- It is becoming almost generic and we are, on a world wide basis, subject to world pressure on local culture 'the global village effect'
- In the micro you only have to go to your neighbours to experience cultural change

The most powerful global influencer of culture
- Is probably film 'movies'
- And they as we know predominantly come from Hollywood in the West …
- … Or from Bollywood in the East

We all watch American movies …
We are all culturally affected …

Why this course is important!
- We need to understand who we are
- We need to understand why we are
- We need a point of reference in any attempt to help others
- We live in an increasingly global world and to understand other cultures, particularly in counselling or other exchanges, our reference points on cultural understanding become more and more important
  - What is Culture?
  - Where does it come from?

60   Culture Clash

- What makes it?

| The Trainer should allow at least one hour for this initial session | 1. |

PowerPoint Number One is available for this session (1)

Expected outcomes:
At the end of this lecture the student should be able to describe what is meant by culture.

Trainers Notes
2. DEFINITIONS

> ➤ A further plan for the trainer to is to encourage the students to find a list of words that explain culture. To do this one could ask the students to use a thesaurus or a dictionary and find words that better describe culture and community and the thing that binds peoples together. Again, a flip chart list would help at a point in this exercise after people have looked things up. It would be good to allow people to work in twos or threes for this session

Some dictionary/thesaurus words
- Civilization
- Humanity
- The world
- People
- The populace
- The community
- No-one
- Each person

The Trainer should allow at least one to one and a half hours for this initial session 3

Expected outcomes:
The student at the end of this session should be able to define culture from various view points.

Trainers Notes

3. THE BASE PILLARS OF CULTURE

> ➤ The trainer will probably find that a straight lecture style will be the best presentation form for this further major part of the introduction to the subject. The trainer should also include reasons why we might be looking at the subject of culture. What is the context of the course? Will people be using the knowledge gained here for cross-cultural counselling, cross cultural teaching maybe in school or a further education programme? There are a variety of reasons why it may be advantageous for your students to understand this interesting concept of culture. It would probably be helpful at this stage of the course to take a straw poll of just why people are taking the course and what they hope to achieve by it. Of course, at this stage they may not be able to express that, and are just aware of the need to understand. There may be those on the course, however, who have met problems in their work, whatever it is, and have been challenged by another cultural way of seeing and doing things.

INTRODUCTION TO THE COURSE

A look at the base pillars of culture
- How they work
- What they do
- The effects of the pillars

It is the effect of family and pressures by
- Politics/Religion
- Education
- Art/Media
- Economics

The four pillars of culture
- Business/economics
- Education/family

- Media/entertainment/advertising
- Politics/government/religion

Are the four pillars on which all culture rests

Culture is not static
- It is constantly changing, though sometimes we are not aware of that fact
- It is becoming almost generic and we are, on a world wide basis, subject to world pressure on local culture 'the global village effect'
- In the micro you only have to go to your neighbours to experience cultural change

Why the pillars are so important

First of all
We need to understand that the pillars of culture are often overlapping and interconnected. It helps us however to see them in some form of separation because we can then think through the implications of each section more effectively so first …

Business/economics
(Pillar number one)
- We often don't think about business/economics as a cultural moulder but it is very powerful
- If you don't have shelter and warmth that will have a real effect on how you think and act
- The advertising industry spends millions trying to sell us things this is often done by persuading us about our image and cultural expression

"The advertising industry often takes away our self esteem and then sells it back to us at the price of the product" *Gerald Coates*

Education/family
(Pillar two)

These two are linked together because it is important to understand that education is not simply going to school it happens in all areas of life

"Education is life" Dr *Donald Howard, American Educator*

Education is Life
During the transition between Rhodesia becoming Zimbabwe the revolutionary forces based themselves in the so called frontline states, i.e. the African states surrounding Zimbabwe, from where they carried out attacks on the country. The most frequent attacks were on schools where they killed staff and took children back across the border to educate them 'properly' (i.e. in revolutionary thinking!). Education moulds culture!

**Media/entertainment/advertising
(Pillar Number three)**

- Are we persuaded by advertising?
- Are we influenced by the entertainment industry?
- Are we aware of product placement in films?
- The advertising industry spends huge amounts of money on
  - Posters
  - TV adverts
  - Newspaper Adverts
  - Product Placement

Why?

Don't you think that in many ways the Media, the Advertising Industry, Newspapers and T.V. are moulding the way we think and therefore are strong moulders of our culture and in fact the culture of the global village?

**Politics/government/religion
(Pillar Number Four)**

- What happens in our legislature ultimately changes our lives
- If it changes the way we live then ultimately that changes the culture or the way we do things
- We often say politics are boring, yet politics enters every part of our lives

Politics and Religion

Some question why we put these two things together …
- From time immemorial the state has used religion to influence and control society and thus influence our culture
- Consider, in the UK, the relationship of the Church of England and the state
- Consider, historically, the conversion of Constantine
- Consider how much religion moulds the culture

Who Are We?
- Very complicated question.
- Our culture persuades us to think in a certain way.
- Culture is, of course, subject to change.
- Some of the ways we think are far older than many of us know.
- A culture comes into being by the four pillars that hold it up which make and shape it.

Romans 12:2 Don't be conformed to this world (allow the world to squeeze you into its mould), but be transformed by the renewing of your mind, so that you may prove what is the good, well-pleasing, and perfect will of God.

The Trainer should allow at least one hour for this second introductory session 4.

The Pillars of Culture PowerPoint is available for this session (2)

Expected outcomes: At the end of this session the student should be able to describe the things that mould and make a culture, and understand how these levers can be used to bring about change for a large people group. The student should have an awareness of how history is continually changing culture by legislation, media, business and education.

Trainers Notes

4. WHY IS KNOWING ABOUT CULTURE IMPORTANT?

> ➢ This next session follows naturally on from the previous session. The trainer needs to try and look further in depth on the subject as to why understanding other cultures is important. This probably will be best done by involving the group in discussion, both collectively (depending on the size of the group) or by breaking the group down into small groups. At some point it will be helpful to the group if findings and discussion is summarised by use of a written flip chart summary.

WHY DO WE NEED TO LOOK AT CULTURE? WHY IS IT IMPORTANT?

Flip chart discussion
- It helps us in our dealing with others
- It makes us analyse ourselves so that we can act and react correctly
- In our multi-cultural societies and cities cross-cultural counselling is more and more important
- We live in a 'Global Village'
- Many of us live in large cities with multi-cultural populations
- We, if we are helping others, need to know where they are coming from and how they arrive at conclusions
- The way others arrive at conclusions may be different from ours. It is important to understand that premise

<u>'Why is knowing about culture important?'</u>

What is Culture?
Where does it come from?
What makes it?

It is the effect of family and pressures by
- Politics/Religion
- Education

- Art/Media
- Economics

The four pillars of culture
- Business/economics
- Education/family
- Media/entertainment/advertising
- Politics/government/religion

Are the four pillars on which all culture rests

Culture is not static
- It is constantly changing, though sometimes we are not aware of that fact
- It is becoming almost generic, and we are, on a world wide basis, subject to world pressure on local culture 'the global village effect'
- In the micro you only have to go to your neighbours to experience cultural change

The most powerful global influencer of culture
- Is probably film 'movies'
- And they as we know predominantly come from Hollywood in the West …
- … Or from Bollywood in the East

We all watch American movies …
We are all culturally affected …

Let us try and look at some of the major current effects on culture
This generation could be called the fatherless generation

This is affecting families and so culture
- In some countries it is due to break up of families—divorce infidelity—loss of stability = pressure of community/individual/culture as a whole
- In some countries it is due to war and loss by death = pressure of community/individual/culture as a whole

- In some countries it is due to AIDS leading to loss of parents = pressure of community/individual/culture as a whole

Many, including governments ask questions that are culturally related
- The loss of family stability world wide—this has huge implications on our culture and, from a government point of view, economics and taxes
- There are various causes of family loss depending where in the world you are
- The end product is the same—huge pressure on the culture as a whole
- What is the greatest cause of family break up here in the UK?
- What effect has family break up had on the community?
- What are the major changes brought about by this pressure of family change on culture?

Here are some of the major cultural changers in the West.
Under Pressure
The Culture!
Historical Perspectives.

What happened?
- Industrial revolution
- Pace of urbanisation
- The last war
- Women's roles
- Fast rate of change
- Cultural change

What was lost?
- Loss of absolutes
- Loss of moral base
- Loss of spirituality
- Loss of faith in science
- Loss of traditions
- Loss of stability

What things have you noticed in terms of change?
- Women's Roles
- Technology
- Urbanisation
- Fast moving change

The following short-hand list is a quick analysis of what has happened in the UK during the last decades:

A Short-hand Look At The Last Decades:
- 40s = war
- 50s = expectation
- 60s = revolution
- 70s = disillusionment
- 80s = selfishness
- 90s = despair
- 00's = ????????

N.B....
New musical express said of the 90s "suicide increased in this decade."
Big UK teen Music Magazine

Who Are We?
- Very complicated question.
- Our culture persuades us to think in a certain way.
- Culture is of course subject to change.
- Some of the ways we think are far older than many of us know.
- A culture comes into being by the four pillars that hold it up which make and shape it.

Conclusion

So why do I tell you all this
- Because if you are to be effective you need to know

- Because we need to understand
- Because we can know where there is wisdom
- So we know why we think like we think
- So we know why others think so
- So we better understand the nature of conflict
- So, where necessary, we can correct our thinking

The Trainer should allow at least one hour for this second introductory session   5.

PowerPoint: Why is knowing about culture important (4)

Expected outcomes:
Students should understand by the end of this session why it is important generally that culture is important, and to be able to say why such a study is important to them.

Trainers Notes

5. HOW CULTURES ARE FORMED

> This session seeks to take the student further in their understanding of how cultures are formed and is probably best delivered via a mixture of lecture style and discussions, interwoven. The trainer is seeking to give the student an understanding of the powers that mould the culture. Under the heading of the pillars the trainer can break down the pillars, sometimes with the input of the group. For example, media will include things like posters, newspapers, film, television, poster hoardings, and the placement of items in popular films. The trainer should look at how the pillars overlap, and should include an understanding of family, religion and the economics of an area. In fact even geography will have a part to play in the moulding of particular cultures. Education of course is not simply that which is imparted formally, though this is powerful, but is, in fact, also received informally. "Education is Life" said Dr Donald Howard, an educational instigator from North America. Politics is not simply central government; the 'village pump' is also a powerful moulder on how people think and a culture is formed and changed.

> It would be good at this point for the trainer to look at how culture is not a static thing but is in constant flux. That flux is sometime slow and so it's a bit like a child growing up. We only become conscious of the changes as we look back. Think about how much mobile phones have changed our life styles and that of our children. What effect has the computer had on our culture? A further useful discussion could be held in this section discussing how generic all of our cultures are becoming. What is the major influence of that process: is it Hollywood and Bollywood, or are there other major influencers such as trade, tourism and travel generally?

DISCUSSION AND BREAK-DOWN OF THE PILLARS

1. Politics
2. Economics
3. Media
4. Education

Where do the different units fit?
How powerful are the different components? List some of the components. Which main section would you put them in and which overlap?

Such as

- Family—maybe in education, but also in economics
- Newspapers—in Media
- Advertising—in Media, but affected by government legislation i.e. Politics
- Government, but how about local effects of village pump politics
- Education—how about Sunday school, Family training, Scouts and Guides etc.?

Culture is not static

- **It is constantly changing, though sometimes we are not aware of that fact**
- **It is becoming almost generic, and we are, on a world wide basis subject to world pressure on local culture 'the global village effect'**
- **In the micro you only have to go to your neighbours to experience cultural change**

The most powerful global influencer of culture

- **Is probably film 'movies'**
- **And they as we know predominantly come from Hollywood in the West …**
- **… Or from Bollywood in the East**

We all watch American movies …
We are all culturally affected …

The Trainer should allow at least two hours for this session and include discussion and report back.   7.

How Cultures are formed PowerPoint is available for this session (3)

> Expected outcomes:
> At the end of this session the student should be able to show what changes they have observed in their own culture over the last ten years, and to show what it is that is effecting such change.

Trainers Notes

6. DEFINING A CULTURE

> ➤ This session should be a little lighter in content. The trainer could have some fun in this session. Often things like food and dress are low key things that people notice the differences in and often can look at with a little more amusement, although there is a serious side to this session in trying to persuade people to engage with culture and understand the big differences in cultural perspectives and understanding. Food and dress lets the student into the more serious side of understanding this subject in a way that is easily acceptable.

> ➤ This session should be as interactive as possible and should use students' own experiences as far as possible. It might be helpful if the students brought to this session some examples of the major discussion items.

WHAT THINGS DEFINE A CULTURE
- Food
- Dress
- Language
- Marriage
- The proximity of others with 'sameness'
- Value system
- Greetings

What are the easy things to spot that demonstrate differences in culture?

Differences in Cultures that are obvious

Things like:-
- **FOOD**
- **GREETINGS**
- **DRESS**
- **LANGUAGE**

> The Trainer should allow at least one hour for this session and include discussion and report back   8.

> Difference in Culture short PowerPoint is available for this session (5)

> **Expected outcomes:**
> **The student should be able to show at the end of this session some of the things that people use to show they are part of a people group 'culture'.**

Trainers Notes

7. LANGUAGE AND CULTURE

- This session probably should have some introduction by the trainer and then allow students time or even homework time to delve into this subject more thoroughly. They could ask questions about language and find out some other language expressions as to how they define certain things for example the Ashanti word for white person is 'bruni' if you ask what does the word mean people will actually say 'white person' however if the word is analysed it actually means a person who has no knees. It's that kind of small nuance that makes language an expression of our deeper thinking in the culture of our language construction. The trainer might get the group to think about words that they use, what they actually mean.

- Language has strange effect on people. I was with a group of young Tamil people in Paris; Tamil culture is a really non touchy culture both in its greeting techniques and its general people contact. On the other hand French cultural is very touchy freely, if you observe a group of Parisians in a restaurant the amount of touching of each other would be statistically huge. So totally opposite to Tamil culture. Watching these young people speaking Tamil, one could see the non touchy Tamil culture. However, stepping in to the group and changing the language to French which they all spoke, I noticed that the body language also changed to feely touch French body language. They kissed goodbye and were very touchy in their conversation. The language changed their whole demeanour. How powerful is language.

- It might be good at this point to consider how our language influences us in things like gender stereotyping.

- It would be useful at some stage in this session to have various newspapers from the different sections of the press for students to examine and comment on.

WORK SESSION ON LANGUAGE

- Consider other languages
- Consider the use of your own language in different social groups
- Consider language as used by second language speakers

- Consider language with the use of body and facial expressions
- Consider young peoples' language
- Consider the effects of text language
- Consider the effects of the computer
- Consider language as used by the different sections of the press

Does language define culture or does culture define language?

> The Trainer should allow this session to include research followed by report back and should allow at least two hours. Some research could be homework based. This session should be at least two hours in length to cover the subject adequately. 10.

> **Expected outcomes:**
> **The student at the end of this session should be able to question their own use of language and question that use, deciding if it is good or bad.**

Trainers Notes

8. CULTURE AND THE CHANGE FACTOR

> ➤ The point of this section is to try and understand how much culture has changed, this might betaken over a period of years. This could be left to the student to decide on how long a period in history they would like to consider, or the Trainer might like to advise. An hour or so needs to be left for the report back on this part of the study.

THE CONSIDERATION OF CULTURE AS A CHANGING FACTOR

Homework what is our culture?—Define it!
Consider

- Modernism
- Post Modernism
- You need to examine how much change has taken place
- You need to think about the effects of new technology on change
- Consider how much old institutions have changed
- What effects does the increase of pace of change have on culture?

Essay and report back

The Trainer should allow about one hour for this session and should include report back and discussion. 11.

There is a short PowerPoint presentation that goes with this session no 6

Expected outcomes:
What has changed over the last ten years? The student should, by the end of this session, be able to define what has changed in the culture of which they are part and what has caused those changes and be able to suggest what could be done to create desirable change in the future.

Trainers Notes

9. CULTURAL CHANGE IN OUR WORLD

> ➤ The trainer will probably want to tackle this part of the course on a part lecture basis, part discussion and part research basis. It may be that your student will be able to come up with lists that are different to the ones below. The lists below may help you to outline the thinking concerning change in our culture and the pressures that cause these changes. Not all change is good for culture, perhaps it would be good to look at good and bad changes and to see what change has done to the culture in general.

LOOKING AT CULTURAL CHANGE IN OUR WORLD
- What are the big changes factors including film?
- What effects has change had on your perspective of life in our world—mobile phones?
- What do you think are the good things about the mobile phone generation?
- What do you think is bad about the mobile phone situation
- Here are some of the major cultural changers in the West. Some of these things will affect you.
  - Under Pressure
  - The Culture!
  - Historical Perspectives

<u>What happened?</u>
- Industrial revolution.
- Pace of urbanisation.
- The last war.
- Women's roles.
- Fast rate of change.
- Cultural change.

What was lost?
- Loss of absolutes
- Loss of moral base
- Loss of spirituality
- Loss of faith in science
- Loss of traditions
- Loss of stability

CHANGE
- Institutional change … it's been huge.
- Technological advance … it's been rapid.
- Material advantage … it's massive

What things have you noticed has changed in terms of:-
- Women's Roles
- Technology
- Urbanisation
- Fast moving change

The following is a short-hand list. It was a quick analysis of what has happened in the UK during the last decades—I wonder if you could try and make a similar list. What does your list look like?
- 40s = war
- 50s = expectation
- 60s = revolution
- 70s = disillusionment
- 80s = selfishness
- 90s = despair
- 00s = ?????????

N.B.…
New musical express said "suicide increased in this decade." '90's'
Big UK teen Music Magazine

> The Trainer should allow about two hours for this session and should include report back and discussion. 13.

> **Expected Outcomes**
> The students should be able by the end of this session to describe, at least from a UK point of view the historical perspectives that have brought about change in the culture of the country. If the student is from another country, encourage historical research that demonstrates change in that country or culture (people group).

Trainers Notes

10. CULTURE AND THE ROLE OF WOMEN

> ➢ In this session the trainer needs to try and get the students to consider women and their role both how they are affected by culture and how they mould and affect culture. One should consider in the West the changing perspectives of women in areas such as work, child rearing, use of money and the law. Plus any other areas that you or the students would want to consider. One should not simply, however, consider women's roles solely in your own country; please try and look at what women do in other countries, particularly in the third world. Look at their choices in terms of marriage, work and education. Consider both their economic well-being and their economic contribution to the family and the nation as a whole. Ask yourself the question: How influential are these women in these areas and what would need to change, if anything, to allow them to be more or less so.

THE ROLE OF WOMEN IN THE WORLD

- Culture effects
- Economic effects
- How does it affect us?
- Does it affect us?
- Try and think beyond the border of you own country for this session

---

The Trainer should allow about two hours for this session and should include report back and discussion.   15.

Expected outcomes:
The student should, by the end of this session, be able to look more clearly at a woman's role in the world and to be objective about if that should, can or could change and what things would be relevant to change.

Trainers Notes
11. HOW URBANISATION CHANGES CULTURE

> Urbanisation is probably the biggest change in our world anywhere. Urbanisation affects all areas of life. It changes the way people interact; it often breaks down previously long held cultural norms. It has economic effects both good and bad. We live in a world of cities, and cities are continuing to grow at an incredible rate. Urbanisation often increases pressure on people; it also means that things like the community are often fractured, or have disappeared altogether. This puts greater need on government, voluntary organisations and people who counsel, as often they are required to pick up the pressures that would have been dealt with by a closely integrated community. Urbanisation, of course, has powerful effects on culture: changing the old and creating a new mode of seeing and understanding.

DISCUSSION ON URBANISATION
- Its reason
- Its effect on culture
- Its effect on Economics
- Anything we would like to comment on
- Anything we think we could or should change

The Trainer should allow about two hours for this session and should include report back and discussion. 17

Expected outcomes:
The student should, by the end of this session, be able to understand the world movement towards urbanization, to discuss its merits and demerits and to understand the pressures of people who live in large conurbations.

Trainers Notes

12. THE IMPORTANCE OF META-NARRATIVE

- ➤ It is likely that many of your students will not know what a meta-narrative is and so we must start this session by using definitions. The simple explanation of this phrase is 'the big picture'. What that means in our study of cultures is this: most cultures, even in our post-modern world (which we shall look at later) use a meta-narrative to understand who they are and where they are in the world in which they live. It gives most people a position. So communists, Muslims, Christians, in fact almost any group that see things in terms of beginnings, middles and endings, will have a meta-narrative that they are working from. That means they will interpret the world around them accordingly.

- ➤ So meta-narrative is very important. Most of us use it without knowing that we are doing so; or at least not knowing about it. There are, however, people groups in our world who do not use meta-narrative and therefore will not see things from our point of view.

- ➤ The tutor in this session needs to get the group to analyse whether they have a meta-narrative and, if so, what it is. For example, a Christian meta-narrative would be creation, fall, sin, redemption, salvation, heaven … or something like that. The tutor will probably find that discussion is the best route for learning in this session. The tutor should also try to get the students to think through what might be the meta-narrative of another group of people different from their own. They might also like to think about what if there is no meta-narrative; how does that work? We will look at that later.

- What it is
- What it does to our world
- What it does to our counselling and general dealings with people
- What happens without it?
- List the kinds of things that might happen without a meta-narrative

The lecture should allow a good two hours for this session and include a report back 19

PowerPoint 7 on meta-narrative is available for this session

Expected outcomes:
The student should, by the end of this session, be able to say who has and who has not got a meta-narrative and to show if this is important in understanding people culture and therefore people's expected outcomes or otherwise.

Trainers Notes

13. OUR PRESUPPOSITIONS!!!

> All of us have presuppositions, yet most of the time we are not even aware of that fact. The fact is we are using our presuppositions all the time, in analysing the world around us. We come to conclusions, we think, on the basis of facts. The problem is that none of us can ever really be totally objective. Our presuppositions colour everything. We look at the facts and then come to a conclusion based on our presuppositions. We should be aware that with a different cultural base, a different set of presuppositions would have been programmed into us. Therefore, when we look at the same set of facts we are quite likely to end up with a different conclusion.

> There are two fun exercises in this section. One is the picture of the young lady and the old lady (it's the same picture). The other is the GODISNOWHERE exercise. It does not really prove anything except that we see things differently and some of us will get different answers and yet be seeing the same thing. It is too simple to say that this is because of our presuppositions, though it might be, however it should encourage the student to think about what they see, what their expectations of their presuppositions are and what the outcome is. Recognising, also, that others come to a different conclusion yet are looking at the same thing from the same angle.

PRESUPPOSITIONS:
- The things that we have that we didn't know we did
- What they do to our perceptions
- What they do in terms of our dealings with others
- How our culture moulds our presuppositions and how our presuppositions mould culture

Exercise one in twos—list as many presuppositions as you can think of
Exercise two in twos—list as many of your own presuppositions as you can think of

The tutor should allow 2 hours for this session and include a report back time   21

There is a PowerPoint presentation 8 on Presuppositions for this section

Expected outcomes: **Students should be able, by the end of this session, to analyze their own presuppositions and to have understood how these are arrived at.**

Trainers Notes

14. OBSERVABLE CHANGE THAT IS CURRENTLY PUTTING PRESSURE ON OUR CULTURE AND CHANGING IT

- ➢ Change is still taking place in our culture, some of that is coming from new and current legislations that takes time to filter down on the culture. Can the group of students look at those things and try and predict what changes could possible take place as these laws and new plans will do as they filter through the culture.
- ➢ It probably would be good if the tutor leads the group through in discussion on this subject and encourages the student to look back through the course at historical things that took place and then later had profound effect that we still live with. For example: one could look at the need for women to work in the Second World War, and the after-effect that that has had on our culture and is still having. What current trends are happening and where may they take us?
- ➢ In this session it would be good to reconsider those four main pillars that mould a culture as there are always things happening in those areas that will affect the future. We need to look at those things and try and assess where and why. By doing this exercise the student will become more aware of trends and movements that will ultimately alter cultures, peoples' ways of thinking and therefore alter the conclusions that people reach in life.

WHAT THINGS ARE THEY?
- Flip chart questions
- Analysis of results
- Discussion in groups
- Feedback

The tutor should allow 2 hours for this session and include a report back time.   22

> Expected outcomes:
> Students should, by the end of this session, have analysed some of today's trends and where they may take us. By doing this they should also be more aware of what people they are dealing with might be thinking and how people's conclusions and thinking may have been or may be being changed. For example, attitudes about marriage might create something different with regard to our understanding of family, be that good or bad.

Trainers' Notes

15. SUB CULTURES AND SPECIAL CULTURES

- ➤ It is recommended that the tutor starts this session with discussion and good use of flip charts. What do we mean by sub cultures and special cultures?
- ➤ It is also recommended that the course tutor uses this section of the course to encourage the student to plan and prepare their own research on the subject. To do this it would be good to split the body of students into groups—a minimum of three persons per group but more if needed.
- ➤ The small group then should decide which particular sub culture they should study and research; and they should decide how they are going to bring a report back to the whole student body. They should also decide how the report will be presented to the group. This will, of course, necessitate deciding who will do what and how. Allow time for the group to decide.
- ➤ Sub groups that could be considered as a special cultural group, this of course is not exhaustive.
- ➤ At this point in the course it would be good to help the students to understand that it isn't only countries, people groups and language groups that adopt cultures but co-operative identities also have cultures: so we talk about the 'culture of the health service' of the culture of 'such and such a business'.
- ➤ The study by the students should include an analysis of a cultural group looking at:-

The making of small cultural groups
- What things make the group a group?
- What are the things that are considered normal to this group?
- Is there any special use of language?
- How does this cultural group related to the macro culture?
- Are there things that would not be immediately understood if you were dealing with this group?

- Are there things that you would be misunderstanding if you had not done a study on this group (for example Ghanaians and showing respect by not looking a senior straight in the eyes in conversation)?
- How has your study of this group helped or hindered your wider thinking in dealing with other cultures and sub cultures?
➢ Foster Children (Children/Teens in the looked after system)
➢ The Deaf community (e.g. people who use sign language to communicate)
➢ Second generation Asians who have been born in the UK.
➢ Second generation Afro Caribbean's who have been born in the UK

DISCUSSION

Introduction to this via a talk on the culture of foster children

This area is very important and one that we often ignore and don't think about; yet it represents a large amount of people. We would like special homework done on this subject in teams to do research and report back to the whole group.

- Need homework doing on this subject

Here are some of the specialist UK groups that we could look at that are not always obvious.

- The culture of Asians who are born and live in the UK
- The culture of the deaf community
- The culture of the blind community
- The culture of those who are disabled, particularly wheelchair users
- The culture of a local company
- The culture of the Health Service
- The culture of the police force (i.e. is culturally racist)

The lecture should allow 2 hours for this session and include a report back time.

30

Expected outcomes:
Students should be able, by the end of this session, to have been able to look at a special group and outline their findings to the whole student body as to what makes up a cultural group and how the group arrived at their accepted norms.

Trainers Notes

16. THE DOMINATING OR DOMINANT CULTURE

- In the UK, and actually in most other countries, there is a dominant culture. Some would argue that there is a world dominant culture. If you are not from the dominant culture then you face extra pressures. Pressures to conform; pressures to move away from some of your own cultural values. This can be traumatic, hard, confusing and difficult to live with. If we are part of the dominant culture either because of skin colour, language, or just an accident of birth sometimes we pay scant regard to those who are perceived to be different. We can take a position that says 'my culture is the norm; it is the right way to live'. Without looking at other cultures, and casting a critical eye over our own in its actions, preconceptions and ways of dealing with others we will be very limited in our outlook and probably quite destructive, even if we mean well.

- The purpose of this session is to look at the dominant culture of the country we live in. To look at the ways it has formed and also at the effect the dominant culture has on other cultures that live in the midst of it; as well as those people groups that become, for all sorts of reasons, sub groups.

- This session will probably be best handled with a mixture of 'led from the front' discussion, all participating, and some 'presented analysis' of what perceptions the students have as to what is a dominant culture.

Both World-wide and In the UK there is a dominant culture
- What is it?
- What does it do?
- What should our response be to it?
- Consider the effects if you are not part of that culture
- Consider the effects if you have an appearance that separates you
- Consider the effects if you do not acquiesce to the dominant culture

---
The lecturer should allow 2 hours for this session and include a summary time. 32

94   Culture Clash

> There is a PowerPoint presentation that can be used in this session: no 9—dominant culture

> **Expected outcomes:**
> **Students should be able, by the end of this session, to have analyzed their own culture and to have understood what a dominant culture is, and what makes it so. They should also be able to demonstrate how that dominant culture might affect other sections of society.**

Trainers Notes

17. WHAT ARE THE PRESSURES AND BENEFITS OF CULTURE ON FAMILY

- The world we live in is creating orphans on a massive scale. Although in the West demographics are moving towards a more senior age of population this is not reality on a world wide scale. Some countries are getting younger as the birth rate pushes down the average age. In the midst of this many situations add to the orphan crisis: in some countries it's AIDS, in others it's war and the use of child soldiers, and often in the West it is divorce running at more than 50%. The effect of these trends means that our cultures are under pressure, and will be changed by these trends.
- The Tutor in this session will need to help the students to understand the pressure on our world of these happenings.

A presentation on the fatherless world

The different reasons affecting the family world wide

- Divorce
- AIDS
- War
- The need for extra housing
- Implications for the future
- Government
- Pensions
- Housing

This obviously affects and changes accepted culture. The current world situation has the most orphans ever. What effect will this have on the culture that we think of as normal?

The lecturer should allow 2 hours for this session and include a summary time.   34

96 Culture Clash

> A PowerPoint presentation is available for this session: no 10—family pressure

> **Expected outcomes:**
> **Students should be able, by the end of this session, to show that they understand some of the world trends in relationship to families. They should also have considered some of the effects this might have on their country and their culture. It will not be possible to be totally predictive but the exercise will have increased the students understanding.**

Trainers Notes

18. SPECIAL GUEST LECTURE FROM 'THROUGH THE ROOF'—PEOPLE WITH DISABILITIES AND THEIR CULTURE

N.B. We have made the suggestion of a special guest here; however it could be any person representing a major specialist group.

- ➢ This lecture will be supplied by a guest lecturer from 'Through the Roof'. 'Through the Roof' is a charity specialising in making people aware of the culture and the needs of people with disabilities. The charity also specialises in supplying wheelchairs to developing countries.

- ➢ The Tutor will need to help the guest lecturer with whatever facilities they need in terms of projectors and distribution of hand-outs.

The lecturer should allow 8 hours for this session and include a summary time.   42

Expected outcomes:
Students should be able, by the end of this session, to have acquired an understanding of one people group who form a sub culture within the UK.

Trainers Notes

19. THE CLASH OF CULTURES

> ➢ This session is a time to look at a particular culture and look at how this cause clashes with the main or dominant culture. It would be good for the tutor to use the research done by the students in the section of the course entitled Sub cultures.

> ➢ The tutor should facilitate the group in looking at how groups clash with the dominant culture.

Consider
- People groups, like Asian, born in the UK
- Speaking two languages
- Where the culture of the home is different from the culture of school or work or dominant culture

---

The lecturer should allow 2 hours for this session and use the students' own research to arrive at conclusions.

Expected outcomes:
Students should be able, by the end of this session, to be able to use their own research of a sub group or another culture and to put this alongside the main culture and draw conclusions as to difficulties created and potential solutions.

Trainers Notes

20. COURSE END/SUMMARY/ PRESENTATION OF COMPLETION CERTIFICATES

Recommended Reading
1. *The Medium is the message* by Marshall McCullan (A look at the media)
2. *Jacob* by Adrian Hawkes (The book covers some aspect of culture)
3. *Futurewise* by Dr. Patrick Dixon
4. *Assumptions That Affect Our Lives* by Dr. Christian Overman M.Ed
5. *Fashion and Style* by Mike Starkey (Culture and the Fashion industry and us)

The world is being transformed before our eyes from an industrial and a technological society into something altogether new and different. Patrick Dixon's book, *Futurewise: Six Faces of Global Change* is a rich and exciting profile of this future from six essential perspectives. The future he sees is Fast, Urban, Tribal, Universal, Radical and Ethical, and in each of these areas, forces are moving that will require wisdom from business leaders who want to thrive. With Dixon's vision, you can plan to change your tomorrow and make changes that will build lasting value.

Hand out material
- Times article on culture
- Power Point presentation on
    o 1. What is Culture
    o 2. The pillars of culture

Recommended Films and Videos
Films you could see that would help you to look at other cultures
- Whale Rider
- East is East
- Bend it like Beckham
- My Big Fat Greek Wedding

- Rabbit-Proof Fence
- Good-bye Lenin!

NB BTI TRAINERS

Add in support mechanisms to students who are struggling. So what specialist things could be added, this may need your careful thought or talk to the **BTI** office.

Our assessment methods to show that the student had understood
- Essays
- Tick sheets
- Assignments

HOMEWORK ASSIGNMENT FOR THE COURSE
TO BE PLACED AS APPROPRIATE DURING THE COURSE

CULTURE COURSE CPD FOR BTI ESSAYS, FILMS, VIDEOS, BOOK REPORTS

ESSAYS/FILMS AND VIDEOS

THE FILM WHALE RIDER:

What does this film teach us about the roll of Woman in the culture that the film portrays and how does this compare to the dominant culture you live in. What change or not should be attempted in your culture?
Essay 1,500 words.

THE FILM EAST IS EAST

This film portrays a period some 20 years ago in UK History. What do you think has changed since then, what new pressures do you think this community or people like them now face?
Essay 1,500 words.

THE FILM BEND IT LIKE BECKHAM

Whilst this is a fun film, what do you think it has to say about Culture or cultures? What did you learn new from the film, what do you like about the culture you are looking at, what did you dislike, how easy would it be to affect change in such a culture, explain.
Essay 1,500 words.

THE FILM MY BIG FAT GREEK WEDDING

Explain the pressures that might be felt by living in one culture but being a member of another, taking note of which is the dominate culture.
Essay 1,500 words.

THE FILM GOODBYE LENIN

There is a clash of cultures in this film, how could we use the example of this clash to look at possible clashes of modern day culture?
Essay 1,000 words

THE FILM RABBIT PROOF FENCE

This is a true story, do you think that the culture of the day influenced the legislation of the time and if so in what way. Do you know what the current implications are; of this film; both on current society in Australia, and current effect for the courts, legislation and the culture as a whole?
Essay 1,500 words

ESSAYS/BOOK REPORTS:

BOOK: The medium is the message by Marshall McCullan

What way does the Medium affect and mould modern culture—discuss?
1,000 words

BOOK: Jacob by Adrian Hawkes

What do you think are the major events so far of the 00's and what effects do you think you see in your experience of Greek Culture?
1,000 words

BOOK: Futurewise Dr Patrick Dixon

The world is changing fast. In this book, Patrick Dixon explores six major trends, that we all need to adapt to Fast—Speed will be everything Urban—how the emphasis on cities will intensify Tribal—conflicts of culture and conscience, for example in Europe Universal—the forces of globalism Radical—the reaction against 20th century values Ethical—a new morality.

What are the reactions against 20th Century Values ethical and cultural, how do you see this going forward in the next 20 years?
Essay 1,500 words.

BOOK: Assumptions that affect our lives Dr Christian Overman M.Ed.

How much are we still influenced by Greek Culture today, and what effect do you think Judaist thinking is present in UK culture?
1,000 words

BOOK: Fashion and Style by Mike Starkey

A look at the history of fashion and how we perceive it—our internal bifocals that due to our culture colour the way we see cloths and the importance of them in expressing culture or opposing it as the case might be. This book is full of surprises.

What are the views of our culture concerning fashion, and what are some of the surprising historical uses of clothes and fashion in Europe?
1,500 words

STUDENTS NOTES FILE

BARNABAS TRAINING CULTURE AT DIPLOMA LEVEL

**Barnabas
Training
International**

<u>TRAINING COURSE ON THE SUBJECT OF CULTURE</u>
THIS COURSE WILL HAVE A MINIMUM OF 35 HOURS CONTACT
TIME PLUS SOME
25 HOURS OF HOME WORK STUDY TIME.

BARNABAS TRAINING INTERNATIONAL

INDEX FOR CULTURAL COURSE

Session 1—What is Culture? 111

Session 2—Definitions 113

Session 3—The Base Pillars of Culture 114

Session 4—Why is Knowing About Culture Important? 117

Session 5—How Cultures are Formed 120

Session 6—Defining a Culture 121

Session 7—Language and Culture 122

Session 8—Culture and the Change Factor 123

Session 9—Cultural Change in Our World 124

Session 10—Culture and the Role of Women 126

Session 11—How Urbanisation Changes Culture 127

Session12—The Importance of Meta-Narrative 128

Session 13—Our Presuppositions!!! 129

Session 14—Observable Change that is Currently Putting Pressure on Our Culture and Changing it 130

Session 15—Sub Cultures and Special Cultures...131

Session 16—The Dominating or Dominant Culture.................................133

Session 17—What Are the Pressures and Benefits of Culture on Family 134

Session 18—Special Guest Lecture From 'Through the Roof'—
    People with Disabilities and Their Culture 136

Session 19—The Clash of Cultures 137

Session 20—Course End/Summary/Presentation of
    Completion Certificates 138

PURPOSE OF THE COURSE

The purpose of the course is not to discover the rights and wrongs about culture, but first to understand ourselves. What expectations have we taken onboard because of our culture? Do we even think about our own culture and what it is? If we live in a fairly mono-cultural area, or surround ourselves with people who are 'very much like us', then we probably don't even think about the subject. It would not be wrong to say there are similarities in English people who live in the North of England and English people who live in the South, but that would be too simplistic a conclusion. We need better understanding than that. If we are using this course to inform us because we are a counsellor then it becomes very important. Peoples' cultures lead them to arrive at different answers from the same set of perspectives. We must be careful, however, as we go through the training set out by this course, not to become so complacent in terms of the acceptance of cultural norms as being ok just because they are culturally accepted! For example, just because it is accepted for men to beat their wives in a particular culture, does that mean that it is right and we just go along with the culture? After all it's their culture and we shouldn't interfere with that should we?

EXPECTED

At the end of this course the student should
- Understand where culture comes from
- Understand how culture is formed
- Understand how culture is changed
- Be aware of other cultures
- Be willing to see things from another perspective by understanding another person's preconceptions

Understand how our
- Ideas
- Thinking
- and Presuppositions

All affect our
- Conclusions

HOW THE COURSE WILL BE ASSESSED FOR STUDENT UNDERSTANDING

By essays
By film reports
By book reports
By analytical report on a set subject within the course

Session 1—What is Culture?

**What is Culture?
Where does it come from?
What makes it?**

IT IS THE EFFECT OF FAMILY AND PRESSURES BY
- Politics/Religion
- Education
- Art/Media
- Economics
- What are the easy things to spot that demonstrate differences in culture?

DIFFERENCES IN CULTURES THAT ARE OBVIOUS

Things like:-
- Food
- Dress
- Music

THE FOUR PILLARS OF CULTURE
- Business/Economics
- Education/Family
- Media/Entertainment/Advertising
- Politics/Government/Religion

Are the four pillars on which all culture rests

THE MOST POWERFUL GLOBAL INFLUENCER OF CULTURE
- Is probably Film/Television

- And they, as we know, predominantly come from Hollywood in the West …
- … Or from Bollywood in the East

We all watch American movies …
We are all culturally affected …

WHY THIS COURSE IS IMPORTANT!
- We need to understand who we are
- We need to understand why we are
- We need a point of reference in any attempt to help others
- We live in an increasingly global world and to understand other cultures, particularly in counselling or other exchanges, our reference points on cultural understanding become more and more important

---
PowerPoint—'What is Culture' (1)

Expected outcomes:
At the end of this session, the student should be able to describe what is meant by 'culture'.

Session 2—Definitions

SOME DICTIONARY/THESAURUS WORDS
- Civilization
- Humanity
- The World
- People
- The Populace
- The Community
- No-one
- Each Person

> **Expected outcomes:**
> At the end of this session, students should be able to define culture from various viewpoints.

Session 3—
The Base Pillars of Culture

INTRODUCTION TO THE COURSE

A LOOK AT THE BASE PILLARS OF CULTURE
- How they work
- What they do
- The effects of the pillars

FIRST OF ALL

We need to understand that the pillars of culture are often overlapping and interconnected. It helps us however to see them in some form of separation because we can then think through the implications of each section more effectively, so first …

BUSINESS/ECONOMICS (PILLAR ONE)
- We often don't think about business/economics as a cultural moulder but it is very powerful
- If you don't have shelter and warmth, that will have a real effect on how you think and act
- The advertising industry spends millions trying to sell us things. This is often done by persuading us about our image and cultural expression

"The advertising industry often take away our self-esteem and then sells it back to us at the price of the product" *Gerald Coates*

EDUCATION/FAMILY (PILLAR TWO)
- These two are linked together because it is important to understand that education is not simply going to school, it happens in all areas of life.

   "Education is life"—*Dr Donald Howard, American Educator*

EDUCATION IS LIFE
- During the transition of Rhodesia becoming Zimbabwe, the revolutionary forces based themselves in the so-called frontline states, i.e. African states surrounding Zimbabwe, from where they carried out attacks on the country. The most frequent attacks were on schools. They murdered staff and took children back across the border to educate them properly i.e. in revolutionary thinking—EDUCATION MOULDS CULTURE!

MEDIA/ENTERTAINMENT/ADVERTISING (PILLAR THREE)
- Are we persuaded by advertising?
- Are we influenced by the entertainment industry?
- Are we aware of product placement in films?

The advertising industry spends huge amounts of money on
- Posters
- TV adverts
- Newspaper Adverts
- Product Placement

Why?

DON'T YOU THINK ...

... that in many ways the media, the advertising industry, newspapers, TV, etc., are moulding the way we think and therefore are strong moulders of our culture and in fact the culture of the Global village?

POLITICS/GOVERNMENT/RELIGION (PILLAR FOUR)
- What happens in our legislature ultimately changes our lives

- If it changes the way we live then, ultimately, it changes the culture or the way we do things
- We often say politics are boring, yet politics enter every part of our lives

POLITICS AND RELIGION

Some reasons why we put these two things together …
- From time immemorial the state has used religion to influence and control society and thus influence our culture
- Consider, in the UK, the relationship of the Church of England and the State
- Consider, historically, the conversion of Constantine
- Consider how much religion moulds culture

Who Are We?
Very complicated question!
- Our culture persuades us to think in a certain way.
- Culture is of course subject to change.
- Some of the ways we think are far older than many of us know.
- A culture comes into being by the four pillars that hold it up which make and shape it.

Romans 12:2 "Don't be conformed to this world, (allow the world to squeeze you into its mould) but be transformed by the renewing of your mind, so that you may prove what is the good, well-pleasing, and perfect will of God."

PowerPoint—'The Pillars of Culture' (2)

Expected outcomes:
At the end of this session, the student should be able to describe the things that mould and make a culture, and understand how these levers can be used to bring about change for a large people group. The student should have an awareness of how history is continually changing culture by legislation, media, business and education.

Session 4—Why is Knowing About Culture Important?

WHY DO WE NEED TO LOOK AT CULTURE? WHY IS IT IMPORTANT?

Flip chart discussion

- It helps us in our dealing with others
- It makes us analyse ourselves so that we can act and react correctly
- In our multicultural societies and cities, cross-cultural counselling is more and more important
- We live in a Global Village
- Many of us live in large cities with multicultural populations
- If we are helping others we need to know where they are coming from and how they arrive at conclusions
- The way others arrive at conclusions may be different from ours. It is important to understand that premise

'WHY IS KNOWING ABOUT CULTURES IMPORTANT'

Culture is not static

- It is constantly changing though sometimes we are not aware of that fact
- It is becoming almost generic, and we are, on a world wide basis, subject to world pressure on local culture 'the global village effect'
- In the micro you only have to go to your neighbours to experience cultural change

Let us try and look at some of the major current effects on culture.

We could call this generation the Fatherless Generation. This is affecting families and so culture.

- In some countries it is due to break up of families—divorce infidelity—loss of stability = pressure of community/individual/culture as a whole
- In some countries it is due to war and loss by death = pressure of community/individual/culture as a whole
- In some countries it is due to AIDS leading to loss of parents = pressure of community/individual/culture as a whole

Many, including governments, ask questions that are culturally related

- The loss of family stability worldwide—this has huge implications on our culture and, from a government point of view, economics and taxes
- There are various causes of family loss depending where in the world you are
- The end product is the same—huge pressure on the culture as a whole
- What is the greatest cause of family break up here in the UK?
- What effect has family break up had on the community?
- What are the major changes brought about by this pressure of family change on culture?

CONCLUSION

So why do I tell you all this?

- Because if you are to be effective you need to know
- Because we need to understand
- So we can know where there is wisdom
- So we know why we think like we think
- So we know why others think like they do
- So we better understand the nature of conflict
- So we can correct our thinking where necessary

PowerPoint—'Why is Knowing About Culture Important' (4)

Expected outcomes:
At the end of this session, students should understand why it is that culture is important and be able to say why such a study is necessary to them.

Session 5—How Cultures are Formed

DISCUSSION AND BREAK DOWN OF THE PILLARS
- Politics
- Economics
- Media
- Education

Where do the different units fit?
How powerful are the different components?—list some of the components.
Which main section would you put them in and which overlap?

Such as:
- Family—maybe in education, but also in economics
- Newspapers—in media
- Advertising—in media, but affected by government legislation i.e. politics
- Government—but how about local effects of village pump politics
- Education—how about Sunday School, family training, Scouts and Guides etc.

> PowerPoint—'How Cultures Are Formed' (3)

> Expected outcomes:
> At the end of this session, the student should be able to show what changes they have observed in their own culture over the last ten years, and to show what it is that is effecting such change.

Session 6—Defining a Culture

WHAT THINGS DEFINE A CULTURE?
- Food
- Dress
- Language
- Marriage
- The proximity of others with same norms
- Value system
- Greetings

What are the easy things to spot that demonstrate differences in culture?

DIFFERENCES IN CULTURES THAT ARE OBVIOUS

Things like:-
- Food
- Greetings
- Dress
- Language

> PowerPoint—'Differences in Culture' (5)

> Expected outcomes:
> At the end of this session, the student should be able to show some of the things that people use to show they are part of a people group 'culture'.

Session 7—Language and Culture

WORK SESSION ON LANGUAGE
- Consider other languages
- Consider the use of your own language in different social groups
- Consider language as used by second language speakers
- Consider language with the use of body and facial expressions
- Consider the language used by young people
- Consider the effects of text language
- Consider the effects of the computer
- Consider language as used by the different sections of the press

Does language define culture or does culture define language?

Expected outcomes:
At the end of this session, the student should be able to question their own use of language deciding if it is good or bad.

Session 8—Culture and the Change Factor

THE CONSIDERATION OF CULTURE AS A CHANGING FACTOR

Homework—What is our Culture?—Define it.

Consider

- Modernism
- Post Modernism
- You need to examine how much change has taken place
- You need to think about the effects of new technology on change
- Consider how much old institutions have changed
- What effect does the increase of pace of change have on culture?

Write a 500-word essay on the above and report back.

> PowerPoint—'Change—Post-Modern Culture' (6)

> Expected outcomes:
> What has changed over the last ten years? At the end of this session, the student should be able to define what has changed in the culture of which they are part and what has caused those changes and also what could be done to create desirable change in the future.

Session 9—Cultural Change in Our World

LOOKING AT CULTURAL CHANGE IN OUR WORLD
- What are the big change factors, including film?
- What effects has change had on your perspective of life in our world—e.g. mobile phones?
- What do you think are the good and bad things about the mobile phone generation?

Here are some of the major cultural changers in the West. Some of these things will affect you.
- Under Pressure
- The Culture!
- Historical perspectives

WHAT HAPPENED?
- Industrial revolution.
- Pace of urbanisation.
- The last war.
- Women's roles.
- Fast rate of change.
- Cultural change.

WHAT WAS LOST?
- Loss of absolutes
- Loss of moral base
- Loss of spirituality
- Loss of faith in science

- Loss of traditions
- Loss of stability

CHANGE
- Institutional change … it's been huge.
- Technological advance … it's been rapid.
- Material advantage … it's massive

What things have you noticed has changed in terms of:-
- Women's roles?
- Technology?
- Urbanisation?
- Fast moving change?

The following is a short-hand list. It was a quick analysis of what has happened in the UK during the last decades—I wonder if you could try and make a similar list. What does your list look like?

- 40s = war
- 50s = expectation
- 60s = revolution
- 70s = disillusionment
- 80s = selfishness
- 90s =despair
- 00s =?????????

NB
New Musical Express magazine said about the 90s "… *suicide increased in this decade.*"

Expected Outcomes
At the end of this session, students should be able to describe, at least from a UK point of view, the historical perspectives that have brought about change in the culture of the country. If the student is from another country, encourage historical research that demonstrates change in that country or culture (people group).

Session 10—Culture and the Role of Women

THE ROLE OF WOMEN IN THE WORLD

- Cultural effects
- Economic effects
- How does it affect us?
- Does it affect us?
- Try and think beyond the border of your own country for this session

> Expected outcomes:
> At the end of this session, the student should be able to look more clearly at a woman's role in the world and to be objective about whether that should, can or could change and what things would be relevant to change. The student should also be able to detail what things need changing to be relevant to women's roles.

Session 11—How Urbanisation Changes Culture

DISCUSSION ON URBANISATION

- Its reason
- Its effect on culture
- Its effect on economics
- Anything we would like to comment on
- Anything we think we could or should change

PowerPoint—'Cities' (12)

Expected outcomes:
At the end of this session, the student should be able to understand the world movement towards urbanisation, to discuss its merits and demerits and to understand the pressures of people who live in large conurbations.

Session 12—The Importance of Meta-Narrative

- What it is
- What it does to our world
- What it does to our counselling and general dealings with people
- What happens without it?
- List the kinds of things that might happen without a Meta-Narrative

PowerPoint—'Meta-Narrative' (7)

Expected outcomes:
At the end of this session, the student should be able to ask who has a Meta-Narrative and to show if this is important in understanding people culture and therefore expected outcomes or otherwise.

Session 13—Our Presuppositions!!!

- The things that we have that we didn't know we did
- What they do to our perceptions
- What they do in terms of our dealings with others
- How our culture moulds our presuppositions and how our presuppositions mould our culture

<u>Exercise one</u>—in groups of 2 lists as many presuppositions as you can

<u>Exercise two</u>—in groups of 2 list as many of your own presuppositions as you can

---

PowerPoint—'Presuppositions' (8)

Expected outcomes:
At the end of this session, students should be able to analyse their own presuppositions and to have understood how we arrive at them.

Session 14—Observable Change that is Currently Putting Pressure on Our Culture and Changing it

WHAT THINGS ARE THEY?
- Flip chart questions
- Analysis of results
- Discussion in groups
- Feedback

> Expected outcomes:
> At the end of this session, students should be able to analyse some of today's trends and where they may take us. By doing this they should also be more aware of what the people they are dealing with might be thinking and how people's conclusions and thinking may have been or be being changed. For example, attitudes about marriage might create something different with regard to our understanding of family, be that good or bad.

Session 15—Sub Cultures and Special Cultures

LET US LOOK AT THE MAKING OF SMALL CULTURAL GROUPS

- What things make the group a group?
- What are the things that are considered normal to this group?
- Is there any special use of language?
- How does this cultural group relate to the macro culture?
- Are there things that would not be immediately understood if you were dealing with this group?
- Are there things that you would misunderstand if you had not done a study on this group (for example Ghanaians and showing respect by not looking a senior straight in the eyes in conversation)?
- How has your study of this group helped or hindered your wider thinking in dealing with other cultures and sub cultures?
  - ➢ Foster Children (Children/Teens in the 'Looked After' system)
  - ➢ The Deaf Community (e.g. people who use sign language to communicate)
  - ➢ Second Generation Asians who have been born in the UK
  - ➢ Second Generation Afro-Caribbean's who have been born in the UK

DISCUSSION

Introduction to this via a talk on the culture of foster children

This area is very important and one that we often ignore and don't think about although it represents large numbers of people. Work in teams of up to 6 people to do research on this specialist subject. Marshal your research together and finally bring it to the student body in the form of a presentation.

Here are some of the specialist UK groups that we could look at that are not always obvious:

- The culture of Asians who are born and live in the UK
- The culture of the deaf community
- The culture of the blind community
- The culture of those who are disabled, particularly wheelchair users
- The culture of a local company
- The culture of the Health Service
- The culture of the Emergency Services e.g. Police Force (i.e. is it culturally racist?)

Expected outcomes:
At the end of this session, students should be able to, along with others, look at a special group and outline their finding to the whole student body as to what makes up a cultural group and how the group arrived at their accepted norms.

Session 16—The Dominating or Dominant Culture

Both worldwide and in the UK there is a dominant culture.
- What is it?
- What does it do?
- What should our response be to it?
- Consider the effects if you are not part of that culture
- Consider the effects if you have an appearance that separates you
- Consider the effects if you do not acquiesce to the dominant culture

> PowerPoint—'Dominant Culture' (9)

> Expected outcomes:
> At the end of this session, students should be able to analyse their own culture and to have understood what a dominant culture is and what makes it so. They should also be able to demonstrate how that might affect other sections of society.

Session 17—What Are the Pressures and Benefits of Culture on Family

The world we live in is creating orphans on a massive scale. Although in the West demographics are moving toward more senior age populations, this is not reality on a worldwide scale. Some countries are getting younger as the birth rate pushes down the average age. In the midst of this there are other pressures—in some countries it's AIDS, in others it's war and the use of child soldiers, and often in the West it is divorce running at more than 50%. The effect of these trends means that our cultures are under pressure, and will be changed by these trends.

A presentation on the fatherless world

The different reasons affecting the family world wide

- Divorce
- AIDS
- War
- The need for extra housing
- Implications for the future
- Government
- Pensions
- Housing

This obviously affects and changes accepted culture. The world situation has the most orphans ever. What effect will this have on the culture that we think of as normal?

> PowerPoint—'Family Pressure' (10)

> **Expected outcomes:**
> At the end of this session, students should be able to show that they understand some of the world trends in relationship to families. They should also have considered some of the effects this might have on their own country and culture. It will not be possible to be totally predictive but the exercise will have increased the students understanding.

Session 18—Special Guest Lecture From 'Through the Roof'—People with Disabilities and Their Culture

This lecture will be supplied by a guest lecturer from 'Through the Roof'—a charity specialising in making people aware of the culture and the needs of people with disabilities. The charity also specialises in supplying wheelchairs to developing countries.

> Expected outcomes:
> At the end of this session students should be able to acquire an understanding of one people group who form a sub-culture within the UK.

Session 19—The Clash of Cultures

This session is a time to look at a particular culture and look at how this cause clashes with the main or dominant culture. Maybe you could use the research done in the section of the course entitled 'Sub-cultures'?

Look at how groups clash with the dominant culture.

Consider

- People groups such as Asians born in the UK
- People speaking two or more languages (where the first language is not English)
- Where the culture of the home is different from the culture of school or work or dominant culture

> **Expected outcomes:**
> At the end of this session students should be able to use their own research of a sub-group or another culture and to put this alongside the main culture and draw conclusions as to difficulties created for a group as illustrated above and potential solutions.

Session 20—Course End/Summary/Presentation of Completion Certificates

Recommended Reading & Films/Videos

RECOMMENDED READING

- *'The Medium is the Message'*—by Marshall McCullan (A look at the media)
- *'Jacob'*—by Adrian Hawkes (This book covers some aspects of culture)
- *'Futurewise: Six Faces of Global Change'*—by Dr. Patrick Dixon (This book looks at the future)
- *'Assumptions That Affect Our Lives'*—by Dr. Christian Overman M.Ed (This book looks at presuppositions)
- *Fashion and Style*—by Mike Starkey (This book looks at fashion from a culture perspective and also some of its historical applications)

The world is being transformed before our eyes from an industrial and a technological society into something altogether new and different. Patrick Dixon's book, *Futurewise: Six Faces of Global Change*, is a rich and exciting profile of this future from six essential perspectives. The future he sees is Fast, Urban, Tribal, Universal, Radical and Ethical, and in each of these areas forces are moving that will require wisdom from business leaders who want to thrive. With Dixon's vision, you can plan to change your tomorrow and make changes that will build lasting value.

HAND-OUT MATERIAL

- Times article on culture

- Culture and its implications for Christian Counselling (*ACC article by Dr. Rhanda Paul*)
- PowerPoint presentation on
    1. What is Culture?
    2. The Pillars of Culture
    3. How Cultures are Formed
    4. Why is Knowing about Culture important?
    5. Differences in Culture
    6. Change/Post-Modern Culture
    7. Meta-Narratives
    8. Presuppositions
    9. The Dominant Culture
    10. Culture in the Family
    11. Accumulative Presentation
    12. Cities

RECOMMENDED FILMS AND VIDEOS
Films you could see that would help you to look at other cultures:
- Whale Rider
- East is East
- Bend It Like Beckham
- My Big Fat Greek Wedding
- Goodbye Lenin

978-0-595-50707-8
0-595-50707-7